The DERBYSHIRE COOKBOOK
Second Helpings

A celebration of the amazing food & drink on our doorstep.
Featuring over 30 stunning recipes.

The Derbyshire Cook Book: Second Helpings

©2018 Meze Publishing Ltd. All rights reserved.

First edition printed in 2018 in the UK.

ISBN: 978-1-910863-34-3

Thank you to: Chris Mapp, The Tickled Trout

Compiled by: Jo Mallinder

Written by: Katie Fisher

*Photography by: Marc Barker
(www.marcabarker.co.uk)
Sam Bowles, Paul Carroll
(www.portraitcollective.com)*

Edited by: Phil Turner

Designed by: Matt Crowder, Paul Cocker

*Contributors: Sarah Koriba, David Wilson,
Alana Bishop, Zofia Filipowicz, Amy Clarke*

*Cover art: David Broadbent
(www.davidbroadbent.co.uk)*

Printed by Bell and Bain Ltd, Glasgow

Published by Meze Publishing Limited
Unit 1b, 2 Kelham Square
Kelham Riverside
Sheffield S3 8SD
Web: www.mezepublishing.co.uk
Telephone: 0114 275 7709
Email: info@mezepublishing.co.uk

FOREWORD

Having spent time away learning my trade in London and Cornwall, the plan was always to come back to the place which I call home, Derbyshire. In 2014 I had that opportunity and purchased a special place, The Tickled Trout, in the village I grew up in. The hard work then began and we have transformed a tired pub into the restaurant I am proud of today.

Derbyshire is very diverse: lush green fields, drystone walls, beautiful rolling hills, valleys and mountains… we have it all. It's not just about the landscape though; we're fortunate to have an abundance of quality produce on our doorstep. The provenance of food is at the heart of my restaurant and it's brilliant that we are able to source simply the best produce from Derbyshire, the glorious Peak District and neighbouring South Yorkshire. The local lamb and beef is stunning, largely due to the exceptional grazing we have; Adam from Country Fresh Foods helps me find the best seasonal local vegetables; our potatoes are grown in the village by Nick Horsely; Kate Brocklehurst produces amazing rapeseed oils near Bakewell; Roger and Susan from Woodthorpe Grange bring the freshest milk and cream every day; the list goes on.

Taking time to forage for the freshest ingredients is something my whole team embrace, and I am proud that my mum's organic garden is the source of many elements of our dishes. Derbyshire has an amazing array of woodlands and streams where you can find all sorts of delights. In spring, for example, wild garlic is in abundance and it brings a unique flavour to many of our dishes. I recommend those reading this to have a go at making their own wild garlic oil.

In a world of commercialism, it is so important to champion local farmers, producers and suppliers. Their tireless efforts enable us to use raw ingredients full of flavour and transform them into a great dish. If you visit The Tickled Trout you will find a map of where every ingredient comes from. The only thing we are short of here is oceans, but I have that covered. My friend Johnny Godden from Cornwall sends his amazing day boat fish up to us, which lands at our door by 10am the day after it was swimming off the Cornish coast.

What is great about this book is that champions of Derbyshire food are collaborating to illustrate the best of what Derbyshire has to offer. Enjoy.

Chris Mapp – The Tickled Trout

CONTENTS

Easy as A,B,C

The Alphabet Gift Shop is a thriving business on a mission to surprise and delight customers with beautifully made, personalised products and freshly prepared food and drink.

With food, drink, gifts, online shopping and an established reputation as a personalised gift specialist, The Alphabet Gift Shop has grown organically in response to demand from the small venture that business owner Sue began at home. The first gift shop in Mickleover in 2008 was followed by the Burton store five years later. Licensed coffee shops now nestle side by side with the gift shops in both locations, and the Burton gift shop recently extended into the shop next door. "We have some lovely customers who have been with us since day one, and then others who have only just discovered us – all people who make it such a pleasure to run the business," says Sue.

When it comes to food and drink, both coffee bars aim to cover everyone's needs throughout the day. Visitors of all ages, even those with four legs, can be sure of a friendly welcome and a relaxed environment where artisan coffee, teas, smoothies and milkshakes can be enjoyed alongside your breakfast, brunch, lunch or afternoon tea. The kitchen uses local produce wherever possible and everything is freshly made by the chefs. Pastry chef Jo is their 'free-from' specialist who has a flair for gluten-free and vegan cakes and treats so tasty you don't even notice what's missing!

The kitchen at Mickleover has a very similar offering on a smaller scale. The cosy coffee bar is tucked behind shelves full of lovely things that Sue and the team have chosen. They are especially keen on local designers and makers, and also have their own range of bags, cushions, aprons and baby gifts which are created to allow for embroidered or printed personalisation. "If we can, we will!" says Sue with regard to making their products that little bit more special by adding a name, date or image in the studio above the Burton shop.

Growing within a network of local entrepreneurs and maintaining a family-oriented atmosphere is important to Sue, whose niece, daughter and sister all work with her at The Alphabet. The aim and ethos of the whole business is about making people and their loved ones happy through food and drink in a great place to meet, relax, and find the perfect gift.

The Alphabet Gift Shop

The Alphabet Gift Shop

GLUTEN-FREE CHOCOLATE ORANGE TORTE

This gluten-free dessert can also be made to suit dairy-free diets by using milk-free dark chocolate and a dairy-free baking block.

Preparation time: 20 minutes | Cooking time: 35 minutes | Serves: 12

Ingredients

225g dark chocolate, chopped

185g unsalted butter (or dairy-free baking block)

2 oranges, zested

60g cocoa powder

6 eggs

250g caster sugar

Method

Preheat the oven to 170°c. Grease and line a 23cm spring-form cake tin.

Melt the chocolate and butter together in a bain-marie. Remove from the heat and whisk in the orange zest and sifted cocoa. Leave to cool for about 10 minutes. Meanwhile, whisk the eggs and sugar together using an electric beater or stand mixer until pale, thick and doubled in volume. Carefully fold in the chocolate mixture into the whisked egg mixture, and then pour the batter into the tin. Place in the centre of the oven on the middle shelf and bake for around 30 minutes, depending on your oven. The top will be a firmer crust and the centre will have a wobble to it. Remove from the oven and leave to cool in the tin. For easier removal, place in the fridge to finish cooling. The top will sink down and become cracked which is perfectly normal.

To serve

The torte can be served warm with crème fraîche, ice cream or a dairy-free alternative such as coconut cream. If serving the dessert cold, it can be topped with soft whipped cream and seasonal fruits for a gorgeous dinner party treat.

Down to a
FINE ART

The Bottle Kiln is a family-run venture showcasing an historic converted pottery and the combination of good food, beautiful objects and a unique atmosphere.

The Bottle Kiln story started in 1983 when Charles Stone and his wife Celia bought an abandoned pottery in West Hallam. As a painter, he was looking for somewhere to showcase his work, and the unique venue just down the road from where he and his family lived was full of potential. A limited budget coupled with a desire to retain its character meant that bricks, tiles and even some timbers were reused, so it felt more like a renovation than a rebuild. The only original part today is the bottle-necked kiln itself, which gave the enterprise its name.

The café took off early on, as people warmed to the combination of home-cooked food and the unusual setting with Charles' paintings on the walls. Under his daughter Rebecca's management the freshly prepared quiches, pies and salads became its trademark, and an oriental tranquil garden was created to provide a little zen alongside the tea and cake. Charles' son Nic took on the retail side of the site, developing what had been a small craft shop into the lifestyle store it has become today, with a fantastic range of gifts, homewares, jewellery, clothing, toiletries and food.

The café has recently seen some exciting developments get underway, including a full refit of the eating and serving areas to give a more contemporary feel to the space and a higher level of service. True to family tradition, the new tables were made in-house from reclaimed timber and there is more exposed brickwork on show. New dishes are constantly being added to the menu, though regulars will be pleased to see their favourites still championed. The whole site is now run by Nic and his wife Linda plus their management team, who strive to combine the best of their own traditions with a generous sprinkling of innovation.

"We are very proud of what we have created here," says Nic, "and aim for it to be an oasis of calm, as well as somewhere to indulge the senses. After 32 years new people are still finding us, but the loyalty of our customers is phenomenal, so we hope to continue providing a unique destination for Derbyshire that keeps getting better and better."

The Bottle Kiln
STICKY TOFFEE CAKE

The original sticky toffee recipe is thought to have been produced by Francis Coulson at Sharrow Bay in the Lake District. Each staff member there today is required to sign a secrecy agreement not to reveal the recipe that is kept in the hotel's vaults! We decided to play on this winter warmer by creating a delicious dessert which can be enjoyed all year round.

Preparation time: 30 minutes | Cooking time: approx. 30 minutes | Serves: 12-14

Ingredients

For the sponge:

600g dates

720ml tea, black and fairly weak

6 large eggs

375g light Muscovado sugar

3 tbsp golden syrup

300g unsalted butter, melted

1 tsp vanilla extract

425g self-raising flour

3 tsp bicarbonate of soda

Pinch of salt

For the sticky toffee sauce:

150g light Muscovado sugar

30g butter

2 tbsp golden syrup

Generous splash of vanilla extract

Pinch of salt

125ml double cream

For the toffee buttercream:

250g unsalted butter, softened

500g icing sugar

Toffee sauce (see above)

Splash of milk (if needed)

Method

For the sponge

Preheat the oven to 180°c, then grease and line three 9 inch sandwich tins. Take the butter for the toffee butter cream out of the fridge so it softens.

To make the cake, place the dates in a saucepan with the tea and bring to the boil, then turn the heat down and leave to simmer for 5 minutes, or until the dates break down to create a paste-like consistency. In a separate bowl, whisk the eggs, sugar and syrup together until pale and fluffy. Gradually whisk in the melted butter. Fold in the cooked dates and vanilla extract. Sift all the dry ingredients over the top of the wet mixture and fold together with a large metal spoon. Divide between the three tins and pop into the oven for around 30 minutes, or until a skewer inserted into the middle of the cake comes out clean.

For the sticky toffee sauce

While the cake is baking, make the toffee sauce. Place all the ingredients, except for the cream, into a saucepan and stir over a gentle heat until all the sugar has dissolved. Bring to a rolling boil and then stir in the cream. Prick the tops of the baked cakes all over with a skewer or cocktail stick before drizzling one third of the toffee sauce over the cakes. Leave the cakes to cool completely in their tins on top of a cooling rack before turning out.

For the toffee buttercream

To make the buttercream, simply whisk the soft butter until creamy and then sift in half of the icing sugar. Whisk the butter and sugar together before doing the same again with the second half of the icing sugar. Add a third of the cold toffee sauce to the buttercream, reserving the final third to drizzle over the top, and whisk in. If the buttercream is too stiff, whisk in a little milk to slacken it.

To serve

Sandwich the cakes together with half of the buttercream and then spread the remaining buttercream on the top of the cake. Drizzle over the reserved toffee sauce to finish.

The Bottle Kiln
APRICOT, PEAR, WALNUT AND BLUE CHEESE QUICHE

We began serving quiche soon after opening more than 30 years ago, and have been producing it in various guises ever since. An absolute signature dish now, it has never stopped being a favourite with our customers. Part of the beauty of this dish is the endless variations, though this recipe is a current favourite of ours.

Preparation time: 30 minutes, plus overnight chilling | Cooking time: 1 hour 10 minutes | Serves: 8-10

Ingredients

For the wholemeal pastry (make this the night before):

240g wholemeal self-raising flour, plus extra for dusting

1 tbsp brown sugar

60g margarine

60g butter, at room temperature

90ml cold water

30ml vegetable oil

For the filling:

120-180g walnuts

540g cheddar cheese

240-300g dried apricots, soaked in boiling water for 20 minutes

120-180g blue Stilton

2 pears, sliced (unpeeled)

5 medium eggs

Full-fat milk (see method)

Method

For the wholemeal pastry

To make the pastry, place all the dry ingredients into a mixing bowl and then add the margarine, butter, cold water and vegetable oil. Mix together – it should be a fairly wet consistency – and shape into a ball. Wrap the pastry in cling film and leave to rest overnight.

The next day, preheat the oven to 160°c. Pop the walnuts into the oven, spread out on a baking tray, to toast for 8-10 minutes. Roll out the chilled pastry on a lightly floured surface to about 5cm larger in diameter than a 30cm quiche tin. Use the rolling pin to lift the pastry then drape over the quiche tin so there is an overhang on all sides. Push the pastry into the corners of the tin then use a knife to trim off excess pastry.

For the filling

The quiche is made in two layers. Sprinkle half the cheddar on the base of the quiche then layer half of the apricots, walnuts, Stilton and sliced pear on top, then repeat this process for a second layer with your remaining ingredients. Beat the eggs in a jug then add enough milk to top up to 720ml and season with salt and pepper. Pour the mixture evenly over the quiche and bake in the oven for 55-60 minutes. The quiche should have set and have a golden brown colour on top. Remove the quiche from the oven and allow to rest for 15–20 minutes before serving.

Sisters doing it for THEMSELVES

Sisters Camilla and Courtney started out by selling homemade treats during their childhood summer holidays, and have come full circle to run their own bakery and shop in Whaley Bridge.

The Bridge Bakehouse is a happy combination of its owners' home town and family. Camilla Digman runs Whaley Bridge's much-loved independent bakery and shop with her sister, Courtney Broome, who looks after the retail side of things while Camilla bakes a blend of classic British favourites and fine French patisserie to be delivered each morning for both wholesale and café customers. Her mum and dad are also involved in the business, and inspiration goes right back to the sisters' Nana with whom they learnt to bake while visiting her in Wales, and would then set up cake stalls to treat other holidaymakers to their efforts!

Before embarking on The Bridge Bakehouse journey, Camilla was a pastry chef with experience of working in high-end restaurants – including Fischer's in Baslow – and the Young Pastry Chef of the Year title to her name. Today she enjoys working with local businesses, particularly the Spar in Calver, Derbyshire which was one of her first partnerships and still has the biggest range of products. Wholesale is a mostly local affair, but also supplies the second largest garden centre in the country, Bents in Lancashire.

The lucky residents of Whaley Bridge can pop by Courtney's shop whenever they fancy a treat or a takeaway lunch. Coffees, teas, sandwiches, savoury bakes and cakes are available during the day from the café to be enjoyed under the awning; the outdoor seating is always occupied even when it's snowing! Local recommendation has been important to Camilla, who is still adding to her repertoire as she experiments with new trends and flavours alongside the well-known favourites. "We try to provide something for everyone," she says, "and most people do say 'wow' when they see the counter, and some take half an hour to choose what they want!"

The sisters recently came up with a new feature to solve this dilemma; selection boxes allow customers to try a little of everything. They also take their treats to farmers' markets and other local events including Chatsworth Christmas Market, and have thought about the possibility of other shops but like to keep the business small and personal. It's all about making the things they love to eat for Camilla and Courtney, so continuing to create great bakes is top of the agenda!

The Bridge Bakehouse
LEMON MERINGUE PIE

We love making people happy with our homemade sweet treats here at The Bridge Bakehouse, and our classic lemon meringue pie always does exactly that! It's been on our cake menu every day since we opened five years ago. If we removed it from our patisserie fridge, we guarantee there would be uproar in our usually sleepy little town of Whaley Bridge in the Peak District…

Preparation time: 30 minutes | Cooking time: 40 minutes
Makes: 6-7 individual 4 inch tarts or 1 large 10 inch tart

Ingredients

For the base:

330g butter, melted

425g digestive biscuits, finely crushed

For the lemon curd:

200g caster sugar

3 lemons, zested

4 free-range eggs

175ml freshly squeezed lemon juice

295g unsalted butter, cubed

For the Italian meringue:

200g egg whites

400g caster sugar

Method

For the base

We've replaced the classic sweet pastry base for a biscuit base in our recipe, having learnt from experience that sweet pastry can go soggy very quickly when covered with lemon curd. Our digestive base is the perfect replacement and is lovely and crunchy partnered with the buttery lemon curd and pillowy meringue.

Mix the melted butter and digestive crumbs together in a bowl. Divide between six to seven individual 4 inch tart tins (or one large 10 inch tart tin.) Push down firmly on the base and up the sides with the back of a teaspoon until smooth. Chill in the fridge while you make the lemon curd filling.

For the lemon curd

Rub the caster sugar and lemon zest together in an electric mixer with a whisk attachment (or just by hand) for 2-3 minutes. This releases the natural oils in the zest. It should smell lemony and aromatic. Whisk in the eggs, then the lemon juice. Place in a medium-sized heavy-bottomed saucepan on a medium to high heat and whisk constantly until the mixture reaches 80°c on a kitchen thermometer. Pass through a sieve using the back of a ladle to push the mixture through. Leave to cool to 60°c. We normally put ours in the fridge for 5-10 minutes. When cool, blend the curd with a stick blender or in a food processor while gradually adding the butter cubes, a little at a time. When combined, the lemon curd is ready! Pour into the biscuit crumb lined tin (or tins) and smooth over with the back of a spoon. Chill in the fridge for an hour at least, but longer would be better.

For the Italian meringue

In a medium-sized bowl, whisk together the egg whites and caster sugar until just combined. Place over a pan of simmering water and heat to 50°c, whisking occasionally. Once the mixture has reached 50°c place in an electric mixer with the whisk attachment or use an electric hand whisk and whip until the mixture is soft, glossy and holds a firm peak.

To assemble

Remove the tarts from their tins and place on a plate or cake stand. Fill a piping bag with the meringue and using your favourite large piping tip, pipe 'blobs' over the lemon curd filling. Alternatively, scoop the meringue on with a spoon and roughly make swirls with a fork. Using a cook's blowtorch, gently toast the meringue, being careful not to burn the tops. You can place the pies under a hot grill if you don't have a blowtorch, but watch the meringue very carefully to just brown it. Serve and enjoy!

Nature and NURTURE

Chatsworth Farm Shop is renowned throughout Derbyshire and beyond for its unrivalled local produce. Located on the Chatsworth Estate, it has established itself as a true destination venue and attracts over one million visitors every year.

Chatsworth Farm Shop was founded in 1977 by Deborah, Duchess of Devonshire, to make Chatsworth's produce available directly to people who want quality, locally grown food. It started off predominantly selling home-grown beef and lamb, but has since developed to offer a staggering variety of exclusive produce from local suppliers.

Led for over 30 years by manager Andre Birkett, the shop is also a fantastic outlet for start-ups and adheres to the ethos that good food begins with quality suppliers. Consequently more than half of all products are grown, produced, sourced or prepared on the Chatsworth Estate. Over the years the shop has helped many new producers and traders to establish themselves.

Openness and ability to diversify has seen Chatsworth Farm Shop flourish into a one-stop outlet for quality food and drink. The in-house bakery produces fresh bread and cakes seven days a week and the deli stocks myriad cooked meats, pies, pasties, pâtés and over 100 cheeses. A diverse fish counter ensures that fishmonger skills aren't lost locally and the extensive pantry stocks cereals, preserves, beers, chocolates, fruits and vegetables.

Beef, lamb and venison are butchered on-site while pork, feathered game and other meats comes from local suppliers. There are 16 varieties of seasonal sausage available daily with around one tonne sold per week. Additional produce – such as asparagus and rhubarb – is celebrated throughout the seasons and served alongside the shop in a restaurant, which also boasts spectacular countryside views.

The restaurant serves delicious dishes created by expert chefs using as much farm shop produce as possible. The patisserie counter is a particular highlight, serving all manner of chocolate delights and fresh cream temptations. All profits from the farm shop and restaurant are driven directly back into the estate; funds go towards the upkeep of the parkland and Chatsworth House itself to ensure that it can be enjoyed for decades to come.

Heritage Carrots
Class 1
Origin: ENGLISH
£3·60 Kilo

Manx kippers

£9.95 per kg

Origin: Isle of Man   Net caught

Chatsworth Farm Shop
CHATSWORTH POT ROAST BEEF

This recipe for slow-cooked, spiced, pot roast beef is extremely popular in the Farm Shop Restaurant throughout the chillier months of the year. It is remarkably easy to make, but the flavours are masterful. Chef's tip: The beef can be cooked a day or so in advance, sliced cold and gently re-heated in the sauce as required.

Preparation time: 10 minutes | Cooking time: 4-5 hours | Serves: 6

Ingredients

1.5kg rolled brisket of beef

40g fresh ginger, peeled and finely chopped

1 tsp ground mace

½ tsp ground ginger

½ tsp ground cloves

½ tsp ground nutmeg

500ml dry cider

30ml white wine vinegar

40g cornflour

Salt and black pepper

Method

Preheat the oven to 140°c. Apart from the beef and cornflour, thoroughly whisk all the ingredients together. Place the beef in an ovenproof lidded dish or casserole. Pour the spiced liquid over the beef, cover with the lid and cook, until very tender, for 4-5 hours.

Once cooked, remove the beef from the cooking liquid and set aside to rest. Transfer the liquid to a pan and thicken to the desired consistency with the cornflour which has been slackened with a little cold water. Adjust the seasoning and slice the beef to serve.

The beef can be kept warm in the sauce, without coming to any harm, for up to an hour. Alternatively, the beef can be cooked a day or so in advance, sliced cold and gently re-heated in the sauce as required.

Let's get CRAFTY

From tasty treats to unusual crafts, it's hard not to be tempted by the range of handcrafted products at the Chesterfield Artisan Market.

Organised by The Market Co. and Chesterfield Borough Council, the Chesterfield Artisan Market is situated in New Square and is held on the last Sunday of every month. It's reminiscent of yesteryear with an upmarket twist, and you'll find over 80 of Derbyshire's finest artisan traders selling authentic, quality produce that focuses on all that is original as well as locally and ethically sourced from Chesterfield and the neighbouring Peak District.

Over the years the market's popularity has boomed, but it's not simply the wonderful produce that attracts market-goers, it's the personal feeling of the market. The talented craftsmen and craftswomen are friendly, passionate, and knowledgeable about what they do and are always happy to talk about their products, which range from knitting materials to natural skin care creams with plenty in between!

Chesterfield Artisan Market also has a strong food offering that reflects this region's love for good grub. For example, Ropers Honey produce natural honey with a unique flavour, and you can also find sweet treats in the form of homemade fudge and fruit pies from Brockleby's. Freshly baked bread makes an ideal accompaniment to a glass of wine from The

Derbyshire Winery for something a little more grown-up; whatever your tastes there are plenty of stalls to dip into.

The traders spend their time baking, brewing, preparing, making and stitching to create an event that people come back to time and again. Whether it's a painting to brighten up a room or a new piece of handcrafted jewellery you're after, there's ample opportunity to browse stalls and talk to artists, vintage dealers and designer-makers, all while sampling some authentic street food and being entertained by local musicians.

Ultimately, this is a market that lives up to its name; a meeting of artisans and foodies who love what they create and produce quality goods. In between the stalls offering up charming curiosities and completely original arts and crafts, the traders bring a myriad of mouth-wateringly fresh, seasonal, and delicious delicacies to your table.

So, whether you're hunting for something that little bit different for dinner, searching for a treat for someone special or looking to discover things you won't find elsewhere, come rain or shine the monthly market will be there to inspire your creative (and culinary) spirit.

One stop SHOP

Weekly markets, speciality markets, and events throughout the year; Chesterfield Market has it all, from your grocery shop to antiques!

Located in the heart of Chesterfield, Chesterfield Market has a long, interesting past. It's one of the oldest markets in the country, having been a trading hub for over 800 years. Made up of a series of weekly markets, speciality monthly markets and a programme of lively events, there is something for everyone to enjoy. Starting with the Open Air Market held every Monday, Friday and Saturday, it's the place to go for a great bargain in Chesterfield, where friendly traders sell everything from cutlery to carpets and pots to potatoes.

It's also home to one of the UK's largest growing flea markets every Thursday, when the town becomes a treasure trove of over 150 stalls selling second-hand and unusual antiques, crockery, vintage clothes, jewellery, crafts and bric-a-brac. Rummage hard enough and you might just discover a priceless antique in disguise! Children are welcome and refreshments are available on site, making it accessible and enjoyable for everyone.

Chesterfield Farmers' Market is yet another regular event in the town well worth a visit. On the second Thursday of every month you can treat yourself to the best local produce, including freshly caught fish, Derbyshire honey and

handmade craft items, direct from farmers and producers. Browse around to find stalls selling locally sourced meat, fresh seafood, cakes to die for, and so much more.

The Market Hall stands proudly at the side of the Market Square and can be seen for miles around. Originally built in 1857 'for the shelter and safeguard of the market people' it now houses a whole host of traders. Pick up old fashioned sweets at Auntie Dot's, browse one of the area's largest selections of cheese at R.P Davidson Cheese Factor, or treat yourself to some of the irresistible cakes on offer at Lamb's Cupcakes.

You can always escape the hustle and bustle of the town centre and wind down with a cup of something hot (or cold) at the Market Café in the middle of the Market Hall, which specialises in both traditional and modern barista coffees and teas. If you find yourself a bit peckish after all that shopping, the café also serves paninis and salads as well as an excellent selection of cakes.

Whichever event tickles your fancy, and whether it's quality produce, a great bargain, or a memorable experience you're after, you'll find it all, all year round at Chesterfield Markets.

Not just run of THE MILL

Cow Close Farm is nestled beneath Stanage Edge in the Peak District, and run by husband and wife Sophie and James Summerlin, who produce delicious artisan cheese by hand, fresh from the green fields of Hathersage.

Sophie and James' passion for cheese was realised in 2013 when they started their own business making handmade, artisan cheeses, which first hit the markets in April 2016. Their hard work starts with the very source: their neighbour's mixture of brown Swiss and black and white cows who live comfortably in their natural habitat. Because what they eat depends on the seasons, their milk changes as their surroundings do which brings unique flavours to each new batch of cheese. It's part of the Cow Close ethos to ensure the high welfare of the animals. The cows graze the fields more and feed themselves throughout the summer, while in winter they are fed and sheltered which actually produces more milk for the cheese-making.

Sophie and James put great care, effort and precision into the cheese-making process, but to create the perfect end product, patience is key. The pasteurising, culturing, renneting, cutting and draining of the cheese through to the final stages happens in just one day, but the whole process from start to finish can take up to 30 days, producing up to 320 cheeses in total. There's always an element of the unknown too, making it

an exciting venture for Sophie and James; a process can be repeated exactly any number of times, yet the end products vary slightly in flavour. To get them ready for selling, the cheeses are wrapped by hand and moved to a cooler fridge, where they soften further and the creamy flavour develops and matures. Once they're ready to go, Sophie and James re-wrap the cheeses and brand them for delivery.

They've named the final products 'Stanage Curd' and 'Stanage Millstone' and both are really versatile for enjoying baked or eaten just as they are. The millstone is shaped like its namesake as you might imagine, paying homage to the Peak District and particularly the abandoned stone relics of industry around Stanage Edge. It's an apt reflection of Cow Close Farm's rugged surroundings and the area's historical heritage, just like the cheese itself. Despite the challenges presented by the unpredictable seasons, Sophie and James are excited to continue growing the handmade artisan business, placing all their passion and love for good cheese into their venture.

Cow Close Farm
TOMATO CHEESECAKE

This is a great savoury cheesecake that can be eaten fresh or prepared ahead of time. Served with a rocket salad, it looks great all dressed up but works equally well as part of a summer picnic.

Preparation time: 30 minutes | Cooking time: 30 minutes | Serves: 8

Ingredients

For the base:

200g-250g crackers (I use Ryvita, but any digestive or salty cracker works)

100g-120g butter, melted

For the filling:

300g curd cheese, at room temperature

150g Stanage Millstone cheese, cut into cubes

2 eggs

Salt and freshly ground pepper

Large bag of spinach

For the topping (option one):

1-2 handfuls of cherry tomatoes

50ml olive oil

10ml wine vinegar

¼ tsp cumin

1 clove of garlic

Salt and freshly ground pepper

The garlic and cumin can also be swapped for basil and black olives

For the topping (option two):

1-2 handfuls of cherry tomatoes

A spoonful or two of pesto

Method

Preheat the oven to 180°c and grease a spring form cake tin.

For the base

Crush or blend the biscuits/crackers (I use a bullet-style multi-blender to get a fine crumb) and then add the melted butter to combine. Press the base into the tin and push up the sides with the back of a spoon. Put in the fridge while you make the filling.

For the filling

Wash the spinach, and without drying place it in a large pan and wilt over a medium-high heat using just the water on the leaves. Drain the wilted spinach thoroughly, and squeeze as much moisture out as possible. This can be done easily in small handfuls once the spinach has cooled a bit. Chop the spinach up a little to avoid long springy pieces.

Mix the curd cheese, Stanage Millstone cheese, eggs, spinach, salt and pepper to an even, soft consistency. Pour the filling over the biscuit base and then bake the cheesecake in the preheated oven for 20-30 minutes before letting it cool completely. The top should be golden and the filling should feel quite firm.

The cheesecake will keep in the fridge for a few days without a topping.

For the topping (option one)

Combine the olive oil, vinegar, cumin, garlic, salt and pepper to make a vinaigrette. Cut the tomatoes in half and mix them into the dressing, then spread them out over the cooled cheesecake and serve.

For the topping (option two)

Cut the tomatoes in half and mix them with the pesto. Spread the tomatoes out over the cheesecake and serve.

A different kind
OF LOCAL

A proper country pub with good grub at its heart, The Elm Tree is a picturesque and unpretentious destination for eating out with friends, family and food lovers in the Derbyshire countryside.

Chris Norfolk is the owner and head chef of The Elm Tree, situated in the little village of Elmton, which has established itself as a proper country pub but also draws customers from far and wide thanks to a well-deserved reputation for great food and drink. Having been included in the Michelin guide, the AA guide, and welcomed visitors who travelled from America and Europe to dine alongside the Derbyshire regulars, the pub is thriving nearly ten years on from its rejuvenation.

When Chris spotted the down-at-heel village local, his first thought was "I can fix that". This was followed by a move from Sheffield out to the middle of the countryside to set up The Elm Tree at just 24 years old. He's run the pub with his wife since 2009 and working by an ethos that is dedicated to common sense as much as quality and high standards.

As much of the menu as possible is made by his team of five chefs and Chris himself. They butcher the best cuts of meat themselves, like to work with game, serve classic dishes with a generous helping of chips on the side and generally produce hearty pub meals for everyone to enjoy. Everyone means just that; whilst you'll find sausages and mash, rack of lamb and even the occasional squirrel on the menu, there are also vegan and vegetarian dishes, plus a section for gluten-free guests and an attitude that's nothing but accommodating towards dietary requirements.

Chris' pride in the food they create starts with the best local produce – sometimes bought from those amongst his own customers who are handy with a shotgun or skilled at foraging – and extends to the informal atmosphere it's served in. Its acre of land makes The Elm Tree an even more beautiful spot for a visit, and weddings, barbecues, hog roasts and more are regulars on the calendar of outdoor events. The pub recently won an award for sourcing locally, and is about to launch another exclusive in the form of a new IPA created especially for The Elm Tree. In "not wanting to just fit a niche" Chris has created a destination that combines the very traditional with individuality and above all, a good pub meal.

The Elm Tree
BEEF WELLINGTON

Customers at The Elm Tree always ask for our beef wellington. Our chef John makes about 25 a week and it's not even on the menu! It's a classic dish but the addition of Parma ham gives it a modern twist, as well as preventing too much moisture escaping when the wellington is cooking; if the filling is well wrapped the pastry will be crisp.

Preparation time: approx. 20 minutes | Cooking time: approx. 45 minutes | Serves: 4

Ingredients

For the pancakes:

1 egg

50g plain flour

50g milk

Salt and pepper

Knob of butter

For the mushroom pâté:

10 wild mushrooms or button mushrooms

1 shallot

1 clove of garlic

Small bunch of parsley, finely chopped

Splash white wine

Knob of butter

Salt and pepper

To cook the beef:

4 x 200g beef fillets

Salt and pepper

Drizzle of cooking oil

20g beef dripping

To make the wellington:

4 x 180g blocks of puff pastry

4 sheets of Parma ham

1 egg, beaten

Method

For the pancakes

Whisk the egg in a bowl, add the flour and get rid of any lumps before adding the milk and seasoning. Leave the batter to stand in the fridge while you prepare the mushroom pâté.

To cook the pancakes, warm a medium-sized non-stick pan over a moderate heat. Melt some of the butter in the pan and pour in a thin even layer of batter. Once the edges have cooked, flip the pancake with a pallet knife. It should be thin and lightly coloured. Repeat until all the mix is used up and then leave the pancakes to cool.

For the mushroom pâté

Chop the mushrooms and shallots as finely as possible, keeping them separate. Purée the garlic by squashing the clove and a little salt with the flat side of a knife. Gently soften the shallots in butter, then reduce the heat and add the garlic. Stir for 1 minute. Add the chopped mushrooms and cook until the moisture from the mushrooms has reduced, stirring occasionally to prevent burning. Add the splash of wine and reduce again, then add the chopped parsley and season to taste. Leave to cool.

To cook the beef

Place a heavy-bottomed frying pan on the stove and get the pan red hot. Season the fillets with salt and pepper. Add a drizzle of oil and place the beef fillets into the pan. Seal the fillets on all sides until they have a nice caramelised glaze. The more colour, the more flavour you'll get later. Once the fillets are on their final side, add the beef dripping and gently roll the fillets in it. Take the beef out of the pan and leave to rest, pouring the remaining dripping over the top.

To make the wellington

Once all the ingredients have cooled it's time to assemble the wellington. Preheat the oven to 200°c and roll out the puff pastry into a small thin rectangle. Trim a pancake on two sides to fit the puff pastry. Wrap the beef fillet in Parma ham and place it on top of the pancake. Add a dessert spoon of the mushroom pâté on top of the fillet. Wrap the fillet in the pancake and then the puff pastry, sealing both ends where the pancakes have been trimmed by folding the top of the pastry under the bottom and pinching the join together. Place the prepared wellington on a baking tray lined with greaseproof paper and repeat for the other three fillets. Egg wash the pastry with the beaten egg and cook in the preheated oven for 30 minutes for rare or 35 minutes for medium rare. Be aware that results will vary depending on how good your oven is.

To serve

We like to serve our beef wellington with creamed cabbage and bacon, proper hand cut chips and beef gravy.

Great balls of GOODNESS

A new, healthy, and delicious snack has come to Derbyshire; Victoria Prince is excited to bring the UK's first recipe kit for energy balls to kitchens across the country.

Early 2018 saw the launch of EnergyBallRecipes.com, a subscription-based business that delivers all the ingredients for homemade treats right through your letterbox. Victoria Prince came up with the idea of creating the recipe kits, with a team of freelancers and her dad on board as chief recipe tester! She first started to play around with energy ball recipes a few years ago; as a chocoholic with a job at Thorntons, Victoria wanted to find a healthier but just as easy option to satisfy her cravings. When the trials worked, she noted down the recipes, and then began sharing them online so other people could try out the sweet treats themselves.

Today, Victoria's venture is up and running following a successful Kickstarter campaign, and recipe kits or gift boxes are ready to order. They contain everything you need – all the ingredients, and a recipe that's easy to follow – to make 30 balls, which is enough for one every day until the next box arrives, if you can ration them for that long! They take ten minutes to put together, don't need baking, keep in the fridge, and even freeze well. For people who like to make food from scratch at home, it's a perfect introduction to the energising, nutritious snacks without having to buy a lot of unfamiliar ingredients that often come in big packs and then languish at the back of the cupboard. As Victoria puts it, "we do all the expensive experimentation for you!"

Part of the aim for EnergyBallRecipes.com is to educate people as well as offering an everyday alternative to mass-produced foods that's naturally vegan and gluten-free. Victoria has a genuine interest in nutrition and a particular aversion to eating snacks whose ingredient lists includes things she can't even pronounce, let alone want to eat! Her sweet and savoury creations have already gone down a storm and Victoria is planning to expand the range as demand grows. "It has the potential to open the door to so many new ways of creating healthy snacks," she says. Having come back to her Derbyshire roots and used her experience of setting up a coffee shop and a deli, she can't wait for the next step in the energy ball revolution!

Energy Ball Recipes
CHOCOLATE ORANGE AND HAZELNUT ENERGY BALLS

Say hello to your new favourite (and totally healthy) snack. These energy balls are packed with protein, fibre, good fats and antioxidants. The raw cacao powder helps to keep sugary-snack cravings at bay while boosting serotonin levels to make you feel good! The idea is you eat one energy ball per day to have a constant health kick, rather than ten at a time (which is easily done, believe me!)

Preparation time: 10 minutes | Makes: 30

Ingredients

10 dates

15g oat-bran

80g ground almonds

1 heaped dessert spoon cacao powder

8g chia seeds

1 heaped dessert spoon hazelnut butter

1 dessert spoon maple syrup

1 orange

15g hazelnuts

Method

Put the dates and oat-bran into a food processor and whiz together until blended. Transfer to a mixing bowl. Add the almonds, cacao powder, chia seeds, hazelnut butter and maple syrup to the bowl and mix well.

Zest the orange and stir into the mixture. Squeeze the orange juice into a separate bowl and add it to the mixture one tablespoon at a time so it reaches the right consistency. You'll know when it's right because you'll be able to take a spoonful of mixture and squeeze it into a ball which stays in place, and isn't too dry or wet.

Before you roll the mixture into balls, grind up half the hazelnuts and spread them onto a plate. Save the other half. To make each energy ball, use a dessert spoon to scoop up the mixture, use your hands to lightly squeeze it into a ball, and then roll it between your palms to produce a more rounded shape.

Add a whole hazelnut into the middle of some of the energy balls for a surprise. As each ball is formed, roll it around in the crushed hazelnuts straight away, to give them the perfect finish.

Store the energy balls in the fridge until you are ready to serve or snack! They will stay fresh in an airtight container for up to seven days in the fridge.

Green or fish FINGERS?

The coffee shop at Ferndale Garden Centre is a family friendly meeting place with freshly cooked food, a relaxed atmosphere, and of course, great coffee.

Ferndale Garden Centre is a family-run business that has been flourishing in Derbyshire for over 36 years. Neil, his wife Linda, and her sister Helen have been running the business together with Linda and Helen's parents who have since retired. The coffee shop at Ferndale has always been really popular, and draws even more of a crowd since its expansion from just 133 seats to around 200. As you'd imagine, lunchtimes are always busy, so the kitchen has a dedicated team of five or six who create the majority of the menu fresh every day, from fish and chips to their famous scones.

The food and drink on offer is based around traditional favourites but dishes are always being added and tweaked so the many regulars always have something new to try out. Local suppliers are a key feature; the award-winning Moss Valley sausages in the gardener's breakfast, for example, only travel about a mile and a half from the farm to end up on the plate at Ferndale! The tempting selection includes a wide variety of delicious freshly baked cakes all made at Ferndale (with the exception of the gluten-free options, which are sourced from a local specialist). It's also gaining a reputation for themed summer specials which match up with a beach area for whole families to enjoy.

Come rain or shine, the coffee shop provides somewhere to relax and enjoy a breakfast, brunch, lunch or treat any day of the week. The refurbished interior has been divided into sections, so the newer area boasts a log burner in the centre of the rustic space, surrounded by up-cycled furniture. The view looks over a sea of green at the garden centre's range of plants, and the deck is a perfect spot to sit out on warmer days.

The garden centre aims to give all visitors an experience that's personal and full of colour, while providing them with plenty of knowledge and a carefully curated selection of plants, outdoor furnishings and gifts. "We like to push ourselves here and are always looking to the future to keep things fresh and interesting for all our customers," says Helen. Helen and her co-owners pride themselves on the lovely team who play such a big part in creating the friendly fun atmosphere that's one of Ferndale's hallmarks, along with the Pollards coffee – roasted in Sheffield – and its fresh, homemade, tasty food.

The Coffee Shop at Ferndale Garden Centre

COURGETTE 'MEATBALLS' WITH PASTA

Our customers really enjoy this dish. It's full of flavour, quick and easy to make, and ticks a lot of other boxes too. Not only is it gluten-free, it's also suitable for vegetarians and vegans. If you're not any of the above, the final flourish of pecorino (literally) tops the dish off perfectly.

Preparation time: 20 minutes | Cooking time: 25 minutes | Serves: 4

Ingredients

2 400g cans of chickpeas, drained and rinsed

180g rolled oats

4 cloves of garlic, peeled

1 tsp dried oregano

1 tsp dried basil

2 tbsp nutritional yeast flakes (available from health food shops and some supermarkets)

½ tsp salt

½ lemon, juiced

350g courgettes, shredded

1 medium-sized onion

500g passata

200g white gluten-free pasta

To serve:

Pecorino cheese, grated (optional)

Few fresh basil leaves, to garnish

Method

Place the chickpeas, rolled oats and three of the garlic cloves in a food processor. Blitz for about 5-10 seconds, until finely chopped. Scoop some of the mixture out of the bowl and press to check that it holds together. Transfer into a large bowl and add the dried herbs, nutritional yeast flakes, salt, lemon juice and shredded courgette. Stir together until well combined. If you find the mixture is too wet to handle, add a little more nutritional yeast to absorb the excess liquid.

Preheat your oven to 180°c and line a baking tray with greaseproof paper or similar. Scoop out a heaped tablespoon of the courgette mixture. Using your hands, roll into a ball and repeat, making 12 in total. Place on the baking tray so that they don't touch each other. Bake for 25 minutes in the preheated oven. Once the courgette balls are light golden brown, remove the baking tray from the oven, and put to one side.

To make the sauce for the pasta while the balls are cooking, finely chop the last clove of garlic and the onion and sweat down in a frying pan. When golden, add the passata and cook on a gentle heat. Place the pasta in a pan of boiling water to cook as instructed on the packet and then drain. Add the sauce to the pasta and turn gently to combine.

To serve

Portion the pasta into preheated bowls and top with courgette balls. If you like, sprinkle some of the pecorino over the dish and garnish with fresh basil leaves.

Two's COMPANY

Fintons Café & Bakehouse is warm, welcoming, and the hub of proper homemade food in Breaston.

Carey Shelton and Louise Finlay met through their children's school and discovered they had a shared ambition to set up their own café. In October 2014, this dream came to fruition in the form of Fintons Café & Bakehouse, which has provided the Derbyshire village of Breaston with hearty breakfasts, lunches, a huge selection of irresistible home-baked cakes, and a friendly welcoming spot for a pot of loose leaf tea or two come rain or shine.

The venture is a collaboration between the two women in every way – even the name Fintons is an amalgamation of their surnames! – and it plays to their strengths and experience from Carey's career in catering and Louise's business background. Even more importantly, though, it's founded on love and passion for what they've created. Carey's bakes are based on her own recipes, or tweaked from those she's inherited or discovered over the years. Her love of baking stems from learning with her Nana, and the emphasis on proper homemade food has never left her.

The café uses a variety of local producers and suppliers for its free-range eggs, artisan breads and other fresh ingredients. The lunch menu changes weekly, featuring different quiches, soups and sandwiches all made in-house. The giant cheese scones are a particular favourite with customers either on their own or as part of a ploughman's platter. Fintons' big breakfasts and afternoon teas are perfect for starting or ending a day feeling well and truly treated. All the food is freshly prepared each day, which also means that dishes can be altered to suit various requirements. Emma, their other full-time cook, specialises in gluten-free food and cakes, and lots of options are dairy-free too, making the café really popular with customers who have special dietary needs.

Fintons marries great food with warm and friendly surroundings, taking inspiration from Scandinavian colours and the concept of a contemporary yet cosy set up. The tables are arranged so you can sit with a group or find your own little nook, plus there's a little garden for whiling away a sunny afternoon with tranquillity (and cake). The café is host to some seasonal events too, and is also available for private hire to celebrate your own occasions. Carey and Louise have always ensured the café is open to anyone; young families and visitors of all ages are among their many regular customers for whom Fintons has a place at the heart of the village.

FINTONS
Café Bakehouse

Welcome to Fintons Café

...ase take the ...to look at our menu
...emade food and cakes as well
... ...ensive drinks menu.

...als are shown on our board
...layed near the till.

Fintons Café & Bakehouse
GINGER WHOOPS

Ginger Whoops was made by accident one day (hence the "whoops") when we had to quickly alter a recipe to save throwing away the whole batch. We now make a Lemon Whoops and a Coconut Whoops too; it's a delicious, flapjack-y, biscuit-y, cakey slice of ginger heaven!

Preparation time: 20 minutes, plus cooling time | Cooking time: 30 minutes | Serves: 6, 9 or 12 depending on how big you cut the portions and how hungry you are!

Ingredients

150g plain flour

100g oats

375g margarine

150g light brown sugar

454g ginger jam

250g caster sugar

4 eggs

250g self-raising flour

2 tsp ground ginger

250g icing sugar

1 lemon, juiced

Method

Use a 23cm square cake tin, either a silicone one or a greased and lined metal one. Place the plain flour, oats, 125g of margarine and all of the brown sugar in a bowl or electric mixer and combine until they form a soft dough. Press the dough into the bottom of your prepared tin. Spread the ginger jam over the dough.

In a mixer or by hand, cream 250g of margarine with the caster sugar until soft. Add the eggs and mix for a few seconds. Add the self-raising flour and ground ginger and fold in until combined. Spread this mixture evenly on the top of the ginger jam.

Bake on the middle shelf of the oven at 180°c for approximately 30 minutes. Make sure that the middle is cooked by inserting a sharp knife or skewer and checking whether it comes out clean. Set the traybake aside to cool.

Combine the icing sugar with the lemon juice and a little water if required to make a thick icing. Spread over the cooled traybake and decorate with crystallised ginger if you like.

Gone FISCHING

The evolution of Fischer's Baslow Hall has been an incredible journey for all involved, with the very best cuisine – inspired by Derbyshire and created with love – always at its heart.

Fischer's is very much a family business, built on genuine passion and impressive talent. In 1988, Max and Susan Fischer fell in love with the beautiful but neglected Baslow Hall, built at the dawn of the 20th century on land that was once part of the Duke of Rutland's estate. The couple, who were already running a successful restaurant in Bakewell, saw the potential for a unique hotel and restaurant in the stately home and its stunning location. They moved their young family and their business to begin renovations and, despite a damaging fire, opened Fischer's the following year.

Max, coming from a background in fine dining, quickly made a name for Fischer's as something quite different to the norm. He merged classical French cooking with a desire to be accessible while still creating an experience to remember, and the result was a Michelin star which Fischer's has retained for over 20 years. Head chef Rupert Rowley – who worked under the likes of Gordon Ramsey, John Burton-Race and Raymond Blanc – joined the kitchen in 2002, maintaining the very high standards that have always been a given at Fischer's. Rupert is a keen innovator, taking full advantage of the incredible produce being grown and reared nearby.

Many ingredients including vegetables, micro herbs, salads, and even some of Sheffield Honey Company's hives come from Baslow Hall's own kitchen and walled gardens, which were designed by Max and are nurtured by him and a dedicated team to take pride of place amidst Baslow Hall's five acres. Going over and above when it comes to the food is down to the flavours and wine pairings in combination with sophistication and excellent service, presided over by general manager and sommelier John Cooper.

Neil Fischer, Max and Susan's eldest son, joined the team in 2016 and is just as passionate about bringing the thriving business into the future. "Our vision is for Fischer's to be a truly fun and exciting environment for guests to indulge and immerse themselves in," he says. Whether they're attending a wine or foraging event, celebrating an occasion, or sampling the Taste of The Seasons menu with front row seats at the kitchen tasting bench, guests will be plied with a warm welcome and the ultimate in award-winning fine dining!

Fischer's Baslow Hall
SCALLOPS, ELDERFLOWER AND CUCUMBER

I chose this dish because it is a good example of the food we do at Fischer's and is an ideal dish for the summer months. Elderflower season has passed for this year, and we always make vinegar and cordial to use throughout the rest of the year. Chef's tips: Make sure the scallops are very fresh, and don't leave them in the vinegar too long or they will go rubbery. For the pickle, baby cucumbers work really well.

Preparation time: 2 weeks for the vinegar, 24 hours for the pickled cucumber and a few hours for the granita | Serves: 4

Ingredients

For the elderflower vinegar:

100ml water

400ml white wine vinegar

100g sugar

30 heads of elderflower

For the pickled cucumbers:

1 cucumber

For the gin and tonic granita:

35ml gin

250ml tonic

15ml elderflower vinegar

15ml elderflower cordial

5g sweet cicely, finely chopped

To finish:

4 hand dived scallops (approx. 50g each)

4 cucumber flowers

Sweet cicely

Samphire

Method

For the elderflower vinegar

Boil the water, vinegar and sugar. Pour this over the elderflowers, seal in a jar and then leave for two weeks. Once ready to use, pass the vinegar through a muslin cloth to remove all the flowers.

For the pickled cucumbers

Peel and slice the cucumbers into 2mm thick rounds. Cover in elderflower vinegar and leave for 24 hours.

For the gin and tonic granita

Mix all the ingredients together and freeze uncovered in a bowl. Once frozen, scrape with a spoon to form a granita.

To finish

Slice the scallops into four neat slices and marinate in the elderflower vinegar for 10 minutes.

Arrange them on the plate, alternating the scallop with slices of cucumber. Season with sea salt and dress with a little more elderflower vinegar. Garnish with the flowers and sea herbs, and then drizzle over a little olive oil. Finish with a couple of generous spoonfuls of the granita and serve immediately.

You scream, I SCREAM...

Italian heritage, four generations of successful family business, and locally renowned award-winning products are Fredericks of Chesterfield's hallmarks, but there's always something new on the horizon for the enterprising ice makers.

Fredericks of Chesterfield have been creating ice cream for over 100 years, making the family business an integral and much-loved part of the region's history. John, the current owner, is the fourth generation to proudly carry the "big responsibility" of continuing this legacy. He has been involved in the business since the tender age of 10, and today there's as much passion and drive as ever behind the company's ongoing evolution.

The journey began at the end of the last century, when Angelo Frederick emigrated from Parma, Italy and decided to produce quality ice cream from his new home in Sheffield. His venture, remarkable in itself during a time before domestic freezers, was effectively the first home delivery service of ice creams in the area and quickly became popular. Angelo passed the baton to his son John Russell, who moved the business to

Chesterfield in 1925 and then to its current site in 1947. Bruno took over the business in 1957 and developed it to where it is today as well. He passed away in January of 2018, leaving his son John to carry on the family tradition.

From horse drawn carts to a fleet of vans, Fredericks is still delivering ice cream around Derbyshire and has also opened two permanent venues to expand the repertoire into other food and drink. The café and gelateria in Queen's Park, Chesterfield offers the full range of Fredericks ice cream as well as authentic Italian pizzas, pastas, coffee, teas, smoothies and milkshakes, prosecco, wines and beers, and a variety of food served from early morning until dusk. It's also available on request for private functions. The emphasis is on quality and original Italian ingredients, though there are dishes from around the world which are all freshly prepared and cooked.

In Bakewell, the café and gelateria serves ice creams and drinks from the counter on the ground floor which can be enjoyed upstairs or out in the sunshine if you're lucky! There are further plans for the future of Fredericks that will celebrate its Italian heritage; John and the team are looking into opening a restaurant and prosecco bar in Bakewell which will serve more of the delicious and authentic Italian food found at the Queen's Park café.

Both venues are really busy throughout the summer, and there's also great demand for Fredericks ice cream at events like weddings, galas, garden parties and the big regional shows and fairs such as the International Horse Trials at Chatsworth, the Eroica Cycle Race, Ashover Show and the Longshaw Sheepdog Trials, Cromford-Belper Steam Rally. The family also have vehicles that charter the history of transporting ice cream from horse drawn carts and old-fashioned barrows right through to modern ice cream vans, recognisable from their jolly decoration and much-loved classic flavours, as well as newer delights inspired by Derbyshire, like Bakewell Pudding ice cream and Chesterfield Pomegranate Aspire.

The ice cream itself has, of course, always been the heart of the venture, and the original recipe that was dreamt up in 1898 by Angelo is the very one that Fredericks still works to. All made at the dairy on Old Hall Road in Brampton, the family's formula is a well-kept secret. "All I can tell you is that when they're making it, it smells absolutely delicious, and the taste is out of this world," says Oliver, the business development manager. The proof is in the pudding, as they say, and those who have tasted the results of the team's talents have heaped plenty of praise on it over the years, including too many awards to count! Silver challenge cups, supreme champion of champions' awards, gold, silver and bronze medals, special diplomas and more are on display at the premises on Old Hall Road.

As for the ice cream, the company is sticking to its long-held ethos of old favourites – tried and tested treats that everyone loves – so classic options like ice cream oysters and wafers may be making a grand return soon. With such an amazing legacy to keep thriving, it's far from just a business to John, who "lives and breathes" ice cream according to his staff!

Fredericks of Chesterfield
ITALIAN MEATBALL SUB

As the company's heritage is Italian, we tried to make this recipe as authentic as possible. This is an absolute favourite of ours, so we thought we'd share it for everyone to enjoy in the comfort of their own home.

Preparation time: 20 minutes | Cooking time: approx. 25 minutes | Serves: 4

Ingredients

For the meatballs:

2 slices of stale bread

250g lean beef mince

1 large egg yolk

1 lemon, zested

½ tsp grated or ground nutmeg

Good pinch of salt and pepper

For the marinara sauce:

2 cloves of garlic, diced small

½ a red chilli, deseeded and diced

Bunch of fresh basil, leaves picked

1 400g tin of good quality chopped tomatoes

1 vegetable stock cube

150ml Italian Chianti

To serve:

4 sun-dried tomato panini

2 packs of buffalo mozzarella

Method

For the meatballs

Blitz the bread in a food processor until you have fine breadcrumbs, and then combine with the rest of the ingredients in a large bowl. Mix with your hands and shape the mix into small balls (about the same size as a gobstopper).

Heat a frying pan with a little olive oil in, and then place three or four meatballs (per sub) into the heated oil, turning frequently until cooked.

For the marinara sauce

Heat a frying pan with a little olive oil in, add the garlic and chilli, fry until the garlic starts to turn golden and then add the fresh basil, tomatoes, stock cube and wine. Let the sauce simmer for about 5 minutes. You should now have a nice chunky sauce. Add salt and pepper to taste, and if you prefer a thinner and smoother sauce, pass it through a sieve. Add the meatballs to the sauce and cook for a further few minutes, stirring to coat the meatballs in the sauce.

To serve

Slice the panini in half and place the meatballs on the bottom half, with a little sauce poured over. Tear the buffalo mozzarella and place some on top of the meatballs. Place the sub without its top half under a grill for a couple of minutes until the mozzarella has melted, then place the top back on and enjoy.

Shop LOCAL

Fresh Basil is locally renowned for celebrating and sharing the finest Derbyshire produce to take home or enjoy amidst the rustic charm of the deli and eatery.

Fresh Basil's owner Charlotte started from humble beginnings when she first joined the deli and eatery as a waitress in 2000. From there, she worked her way up to the general manager, and then bought the business herself in 2015. The current manager, Adam, has been a friend of hers for many years and helps keeps the business moving in a direction they are both really proud of. Fresh Basil uses a network of local suppliers and independents to sell a huge range of food and drink; the venture is all about high quality products as well as supporting the local community of producers and artisans.

The deli and eatery is a lovely place to relax over breakfast or lunch thanks to the friendly welcome and a menu that's guaranteed to be good, since it's created out of the fantastic products sold in the deli. Tapas boards and daily specials keep the choices as fresh as the meals, which are all made in Fresh Basil's kitchen. It's been awarded Derbyshire's Best Breakfast three years running and showcases meats from the local butcher and breads, scones, cakes and more sweet treats from local bakers in a mouth-watering window display.

If one helping just isn't enough, you can of course take away the cakes and other products from the deli side of Fresh Basil. A bespoke hamper makes for a unique gift or treat, and can be filled with wine, artisan breads, jams and chutneys, meats, and cheeses according to your taste and budget. Speaking of cheeses, Fresh Basil's cold counter has over 100 varieties available and access to over 5000! You could even put together a pre-made picnic box with one of the baskets that adorn the shop front and its signature Pashley bicycle, giving the deli an old-fashioned country vibe that's as inviting as the edibles.

When she became Fresh Basil's owner, Charlotte didn't want to change too much about the business because it was already so well-loved by established regulars who have continued to visit over the years, but she has added to its appeal by introducing new aspects. Occasional evening openings feature themed food and live music, and Fresh Basil now offers outside catering for private events such as parties or weddings across Derbyshire. Both champion the same wonderful local food and drink available in the deli and eatery, which Fresh Basil continues to celebrate and thrive on.

A local love AFFAIR

Siobhan and Graham have brought a whole lot of love to The George along with a vision for eating and drinking that marries class and style with a friendly welcome.

The George is a picturesque pub in the village of Alstonefield, surrounded by beautiful countryside which provides produce and inspiration for the food and drink served there. Owners Siobhan and Graham are local to the area, and were fond of dinner and a drink at The George even before the opportunity to buy it came along in 2017. Siobhan works full-time as well as being the resident foodie and marketing whizz at The George, and her husband Graham brings his considerable experience managing a renowned restaurant and pubs to the party.

They have a well-established, award-winning team who have been putting their talents and hard work into the pub for many years. It's really important to Siobhan and Graham that people enjoy working at The George, and that caring approach has translated into a really positive atmosphere there for both staff and customers. Above all, Siobhan and Graham want to offer a place to eat and drink that's friendly and accessible. They have a strong vision for the food and drink too, and want to make their own mark – rather than "trying to be everything to everyone," explains Siobhan – by accentuating the combination of really good food in a cosy setting.

The main ethos at The George is about creating an all-round lovely experience, from the food to the service. All the dishes on the lunch, dinner, and tasting menus are made on the premises with ingredients sourced wherever possible within a 15 mile radius. It's important to Siobhan, Graham, and the kitchen team that the food offering "stays true to the environment" which means maintaining a natural relationship to the produce they work with. The pork, for example, comes from Gloucester Old Spot pigs that are raised with welfare and environmental conservation at the forefront of the farmer's concerns.

The George will soon boast its very own kitchen garden, which is being reinstated in collaboration with local farmers and plant nurseries. The balance between seasonally led and creative cooking is a crucial part of the principles that Siobhan and Graham have stuck by, as they continue to develop The George into a unique destination that they are passionate about and proud of.

The George
TEMPURA SOFT SHELL CRAB
WITH BLOODY MARY GAZPACHO

Kelvin and I love this dish; it simply screams out summer and is by far one of our best sellers. The combination of crispy soft shell, dressed crab meat and our Bloody Mary gazpacho is one that customers never fail to rave over. The locally sourced heritage tomatoes we use in this dish are some of The George's most prized local ingredient this time of year and never escape our menu. They are always supplied by our local veg supplier, Bob in Ashbourne.

Preparation time: 45-60 minutes | Cooking time: 15 minutes | Serves: 6

Ingredients

For the gazpacho:

3 ripe plum tomatoes

1 large red pepper

½ cucumber

½ red chilli, deseeded

2 sticks of celery

½ red onion

250ml tomato juice

Splash of vodka (to taste, optional)

8 good splashes of Worcestershire sauce

1 lemon, juiced

Salt and black pepper

Few drops of Tabasco

For the tempura batter:

150g plain flour, plus extra for dusting

100g cornflour

50g baking powder

Soda water

For the tomato salad:

4 heritage tomatoes (different colours look stunning)

Drizzle of olive oil

1 clove of garlic, crushed

A few basil leaves, torn

For the crab:

200g white Devon crab claw meat (other white crab meat will do fine)

1 tbsp crème fraîche

1 tbsp chopped chives

3 soft shell crabs, cut in half

Method

For the gazpacho

Combine all the ingredients for the gazpacho in a blender till smooth, then pass through a fine sieve and store in the fridge until ready for plating.

For the tempura batter

Next, make the tempura batter by sieving the flours and baking powder together and then whisking in enough soda water to make a light batter. This needs at least half an hour to rest before use, to allow the baking powder in the batter to settle.

For the tomato salad

Cut the tomatoes into bite-size wedges; we like to cut them into different shapes to give the dish a bit more finesse. Put them all into a bowl, drizzle with olive oil, then add the crushed garlic clove, torn basil leaves, and salt and pepper. Gently mix and then leave to marinate for half an hour to let the tomatoes absorb all that lovely flavour.

For the crab

Mix the white crab meat with the crème fraîche and chives, then add lemon juice and seasoning to taste. Make sure there are no small pieces of crab shell still in there, then set aside in the fridge.

Now set a fryer to 180°c. Coat the soft shell crab pieces in the extra flour, then drop them into the tempura batter. Gently shake off any excess batter and then carefully place them into the hot fryer. The crabs should take about 1½ minutes on each side till golden brown then take out and let them drain on a paper towel.

To serve

To plate, ladle a good helping of gazpacho into a bowl then arrange the marinated tomatoes around the edge, making sure to dab off excess oil with a paper towel. Add a small quenelle of the crab meat, then half a soft shell crab, and finish with a couple of basil leaves and a drizzle of your tomato marinade.

The George
RHUBARB AND GINGER

Rhubarb is a fruit we love to use here at The George. The "forced" rhubarb emerges in February, and we continue to cook with this delicious ingredient through to the summer months when it grows naturally. For this recipe, I'm going back to my Yorkshire roots and using classic flavours of rhubarb and ginger.

Preparation time: 1 hour, plus 5 hours chilling | Cooking time: 1 hour 40 minutes | Serves: 8

Ingredients

For the rhubarb purée:

2kg rhubarb

200g sugar

For Nana's ginger parkin:

55g butter

110g black treacle

225g self-raising flour

1 tsp bicarbonate of soda

1 tsp ground ginger

110g caster sugar

1 egg

200ml milk

For the rhubarb cheesecake:

300g white chocolate

300g mascarpone cheese

125g rhubarb purée (see above)

For the rhubarb jelly:

3.5g agar agar

¼ tsp caster sugar

450ml rhubarb juice

For the poached rhubarb:

2 rhubarb sticks

100g caster sugar

For the rhubarb sorbet:

1 leaf of gelatine

375g rhubarb purée (see above)

175g caster sugar

30g trimoline

Method

For the rhubarb purée

Wash the rhubarb and then place the ingredients in a pan with 200ml of water. Bring to a simmer, stirring occasionally. Blend and pass through a fine sieve.

For Nana's ginger parkin

Preheat the oven to 150°c. Grease and line a 20cm baking tin. Gently heat the butter and black treacle in a pan until melted. Sieve the flour, bicarbonate of soda and ginger into a large bowl. Stir in the caster sugar. Make a well in the flour and then gradually pour in the butter treacle mixture, stirring as you pour to combine. Beat the egg and milk together then pour into the flour mixture, mixing to a smooth consistency. Transfer the parkin mixture to the prepared tin and bake in the preheated oven for 45 minutes to 1 hour or until a skewer comes out clean. Leave to cool on a wire rack, then turn out and slice the parkin horizontally to the desired thickness of your cheesecake base. Using the individual moulds as templates, cut the parkin into portions (or you could use the 20cm baking tin to make one large cheesecake). Any remaining pieces can be dried out or blitzed to a crumb for use in the presentation of the dish.

For the rhubarb cheesecake and rhubarb jelly

Melt the chocolate in a glass bowl over a pan of simmering water. Beat the mascarpone cheese and the rhubarb purée together, then add the melted chocolate and stir to combine. Pour the mixture into moulds, leaving a slight gap for the topping. Leave to set in the fridge for 3-5 hours. For the rhubarb jelly stir the agar into the caster sugar. Bring the rhubarb juice to the boil and then whisk in the agar mix. Bring back to the boil then take off the heat. Leave to cool slightly before pouring the jelly onto the cheesecakes, filling each mould. Set in the fridge. Any remaining jelly can be puréed to make a gel and used for presentation.

For the poached rhubarb

Preheat the oven to 130°c. Cut the rhubarb sticks into 8cm pieces, then half them lengthways. Place in a large oven tray. Put the sugar into a pan with 200ml of water; bring to a simmer until the sugar has dissolved. Pour the sugar syrup over the rhubarb, then cling film the tray tightly. Place the tray in the oven and cook the rhubarb for 20 minutes until soft.

For the rhubarb sorbet

Soak the gelatine in cold water. Put other ingredients into a pan with 125ml of water and bring to a simmer. Add the gelatine and stir until dissolved. Leave to cool. Transfer the mixture into an ice cream machine and churn until it has a thick whipped consistency. Freeze.

To serve

Place the poached rhubarb pieces to one side of the plate along with a spoonful of the gel. Add a slice of the cheesecake, some parkin crumb and finally a quenelle of the rhubarb sorbet.

Nose to TAIL

Ginger Butchers is a family business with a totally hands-on approach when it comes to quality produce, driven by a committed team of people whose work is not just a job, but a lifestyle.

The Armstrongs – Jim, Gill, Tom and Ed – are farmers and butchers with a genuine passion for what they do. Now in its fourth generation, the family business is thriving as more people choose to eat better quality meat and provenance is a bigger concern along with animal welfare. The Ginger Butchers, as the red-headed bunch are known, can proudly attest to the quality and provenance of all their products since everything is prepared and reared by the family on their farm, or sourced from other farmers they know in the area, and sold in their own shop on Bakewell's Granby Road.

New Close Farm is where all the action happens, from raising Gloucester Old Spot and Welsh pigs to dry-curing bacon and making sausages by hand. The family home and business sits in the heart of White Peak's rich grazing pastures, on the edge of Over Haddon. All the meat from home-reared or local cattle, sheep and pigs is matured before being butchered with expertise that has been handed down over the years of experience in the family. Tom manages the butchery side of the business while his dad Jim oversees the farm and the business as a whole, mum Gill deals with finance, and Ed

looks after the shop, so everyone has a crucial role to play. "I was absolutely delighted when the boys asked to join the business," says Jim. "We don't know of another butcher doing the same thing as us, and we're very proud of everything the business achieves."

Tom and Ed also run an outside catering company, Ginger Cooks, where hog roasts, barbecues, and carveries become the star of the show. The brothers are happy to be "adventurous and creative" for any occasion so each individual gets a slap-up meal to remember. The family ethos carries through all aspects of the business, in the way they look after their animals, the skills used in the butchery, and always meeting the high standards they set, down to using every part of the animal possible in their pies, potted meat, dripping, pastries and other award-winning baked goods. The Armstrong family and their team's intentions are ultimately to ensure that everything they do is of the very best quality; from nose to tail their business is tailor-made with love, care, and plenty of pride.

Ginger Butchers
STUFFED CHICKEN BREAST WITH STREAKY BACON

This recipe was created by one of our longstanding members of staff. It is one of our best sellers and is extremely quick and easy to make. Due to its popularity, we recently entered it into the Smithfield Awards where it won gold; judge's comments included "one of the best products I've tasted today"!

Preparation time: 15 minutes | Cooking time: 35 minutes | Serves: 2

Ingredients

2 skinless chicken breasts (approx. 170g each)

10g fresh basil, plus a couple of leaves for decoration

20g sun-dried tomatoes

30g cream cheese and chive

8 rashers of thinly sliced streaky bacon

Method

Preheat the oven to 180°c and then prepare the chicken by cutting small pockets in the thickest part of the breasts. Finely chop the basil and sun-dried tomatoes, and then mix the cream cheese and chive with the chopped basil and sun-dried tomatoes. Fill the pockets with the mixture.

Lay out the rashers of streaky bacon, each slightly overlapping the next. Criss-cross the bacon over the breast and lay a basil leaf on top for decoration. Bake in the preheated oven for 35 minutes, until the juices from the chicken are clear and the bacon is crispy.

To serve

We recommend serving the stuffed chicken breasts with steamed new potatoes and asparagus. Enjoy!

Keeping it in THE FAMILY

Granny Mary's Original Recipes are just what it says on the tin: great food, made to the standards set in 1927 by Granny Mary herself, with the best ingredients and absolutely nothing artificial.

Original Recipes was founded in 2012 by Will and Alistair Sutherland, who have a deep-rooted connection to the products they are recreating. Popularly known as Granny Mary's, the company set out to continue the legacy of Mary and Eddie Sutherland, who set up their own business in 1920s' Sheffield by selling potted beef – made by Mary to a secret recipe concocted at their home on Tavistock Road – all over the north of England. Alistair and his son Will decided to work by the same ethos as their Granny and Great-Granny, not using anything that wouldn't have been available to Mary in 1927 and putting absolutely nothing artificial into their pâtés, spreads, dips, sauces and other ranges made in Chesterfield today.

You can find Granny Mary's products in farm shops as well as at many of the regional food fairs and farmers' markets across Derbyshire. Will is a regular at weekend events such as Bakewell Market, as part of a team who are all passionate about the great food they make and sell together. Alistair was helping to make potted beef by the age of seven, and had continued to reproduce the delicacy for family and friends until Will's enthusiasm for setting up the company persuaded him to start the journey towards reinstating the Sutherlands' reputation for quality produce in Yorkshire and Derbyshire and passing on his all-important expertise.

"If we're going to do it, we're going to do it properly," was their motto from the beginning, and remains true as the company continues to grow. Proper British meals with vegetable side dishes sit alongside an ever-expanding range of products made with the best ingredients they can find – which means sourcing the tastiest cuts from local butchers, such as brisket for their flagship potted beef – and the love and care passed down through the generations of a family who know about great food. The Pro Chef range recently joined the line-up, which provides pâtés and terrines for the food service industry at a professional level.

Whatever they turn their hand to, the Sutherland family aim to deliver a standard of quality and honesty that's never compromised. From Mary's original recipes, to a place in today's competitive market, Original Recipes stands out in a crowd thanks to generous helpings of expertise, passion, and dedication to the family ethos that began the whole story.

Time for TEA

Quaint, authentic, and homely just about sum up the H&F Vintage Tearooms in Chesterfield; a slice of yesteryear you won't want to miss.

The concept behind Chesterfield's H&F Vintage Tearooms is quirky and charming, just like its décor. Louise Peel, owner of H&F Furniture, initially came up with the idea of opening a small café within her furniture shop with a vintage, homely theme. Soon enough, the café became a destination in its own right and no longer relied on the furniture shop for all its customers. Today Louise still owns H&F Furniture, but when the opportunity arose to buy the café, Sharon Hilton jumped at it. The shop and the café still remain very close as friends and as businesses, each bringing custom for the other.

"It's quite family-oriented here. My son is a shareholder, my daughter works here and my grandchildren regularly visit for the cakes and milkshakes!" says Sharon. Her team are close-knit too, with chef Shane and bakers Amy and Victoria working in the open kitchen so customers can see the variety of cakes and sweet treats being made. Other highlights from the tearoom menu include afternoon teas featuring scones with jam and clotted cream, all served on vintage china by waitresses who dress the part in 40s attire.

With a focus on their array of cakes and loose leaf teas, Sharon likes to keep their menu small and light, and all of their ingredients are locally sourced and from a nearby greengrocer and farmer. The tearooms host special evening events that can range from wood-fired pizza to 1940s entertainment. It's ideal for occasions, as the tearoom is available to hire for parties from weddings to baby-showers, and Sharon will happily accommodate any special dietary requirements, including vegan and gluten-free diets, and create bespoke cakes to suit the occasion. Afternoon tea gift vouchers are also available, and the tearooms are fully licenced so you can celebrate with prosecco, gins, wines and bottled beers alongside your tea and cake!

With its cosy interior, mismatched crockery, and traditional menu, H&F Vintage Tearooms are a step back into the nostalgic past and a sanctuary from the hustle of bustle of modern life. There's always time for tea and cake; the only worry is which to choose! The array of old favourites and new additions on the cake counter is always evolving, but for Sharon, chocolate Guinness cake will always prevail.

H&F Vintage Tearooms
CHOCOLATE GUINNESS CAKE

This is a rich, moist cake that's perfect served on its own, or with some juicy strawberries on the side. The chocolate flavour is really brought out by the Guinness. It's my favourite of all the cakes we make here at the tearooms and is simply delicious!

Preparation time: 30 minutes | Cooking time: approx. 1 hour | Serves: 12-14

Ingredients

For the cake:

250ml Guinness

250g salted butter

75g cocoa powder

400g caster sugar

150ml sour cream

2 eggs

1 tbsp vanilla extract

280g self-raising flour

2 tsp bicarbonate of soda

For the topping:

200g cream cheese

50ml double cream

100g icing sugar

Method

Preheat the oven to 160°c and grease and line a 23cm cake tin.

For the cake

Put the Guinness and butter in a microwavable bowl and heat until melted. Add the cocoa powder and sugar to the bowl and whisk until combined. Put the sour cream, eggs and vanilla in a separate bowl and mix well. Add this to the Guinness mixture and stir. Finally, add the sieved flour and bicarbonate of soda to the bowl and mix until you have a smooth, velvety batter. Transfer into the cake tin and place in the oven for 50-55 minutes, until a skewer inserted into the centre of the cake comes out clean. When the cake is done, remove from the oven and place on a cooling rack until completely cold.

For the topping

Put the cream cheese, double cream and icing sugar into a bowl and mix until thoroughly combined. The mixture should have the consistency of whipped cream. Spread over the top of the cooled cake and use a palette knife to swirl the topping around so it looks like beer froth. The finished cake will keep for a week in an airtight container, or two weeks without the topping.

The ride of
YOUR LIFE

Hassop Station is a thriving revival of the former railway station on the Monsal Trail, offering a destination for cyclists, hikers, families, book lovers and visitors who fancy a spot of lunch or an evening meal surrounded by the beauty of the Peak District.

Duncan and Rebecca Stokes have created a destination for Derbyshire to be proud of with their focus on "food, family and fresh air" at Hassop Station. The husband and wife team took on the renovation of the abandoned station building with two kids of their own and a love of the county they were born and bred in. The family were riding bikes along the Monsal Trail when they came across the dilapidated former station building in 2010; it wasn't long after that their new venture began with a café and book shop in the fully refurbished space. The reopening of the Monsal tunnels in 2011 gave the trail a new lease of life, and Hassop Station has since evolved to include cycle hire and repair facilities, an electric bike showroom, a children's play area, gift shop, a covered courtyard for al fresco eating whatever weather the Peaks bring, and food whose reputation goes before it.

Hassop Station's café can serve up to a few hundred visitors at its busiest, but the standard of food and the ethos the team work by is always consistent because the owners are committed to staying true to their home ties. Produce is sourced from nearby suppliers and producers for Hassop Station's kitchen, not because it's the on-trend thing to do but because Duncan and Rebecca see their business as a continuing and integral part of the Derbyshire economy, so it just makes good sense to look after one another, such as the butcher with whom they went to school! "Our food drives the business all year round," says Duncan, "and we like to be able to hold our heads up high and support the locals too."

His team of chefs, led by Graham Mitchell, are a longstanding part of Hassop Station's success. They produce the familiar café menu of tasty, traditional classics that regular visitors know and love, as well as the stonebaked pizzas, seafood and mezze platters, and range of burgers on the more recently introduced evening menu. For the Stokes, it's about keeping the simple things without compromising on quality and flavour. They're celebrating their own piece of the "golden triangle" between Chatsworth House, Bakewell and Monsal Head with plenty of food, an award-winning family-friendly welcome and the fresh air of this unique spot in the Derbyshire countryside.

Hassop Station Café
TANDOORI CHICKEN FLATBREAD

We had this dish on our summer evening menu last year, and as we like to change the evening menu each year we didn't put it on this time. However, after the amount of requests we had on the first few evenings we decided to put it back on! Once again, it's now our most popular evening dish.

Preparation time: 15 minutes plus 24 hours marinating and 30 minutes proving
Cooking time: 15 minutes | Serves: 2

Ingredients

For the tandoori kebab:

1 tsp cumin

1 tsp coriander

½ tsp chilli powder

1 tsp turmeric

280ml natural yoghurt, plus extra for serving

20g fresh ginger, grated

½ lemon, zest and juice

2 cloves of garlic, puréed

Pinch of salt

Red colouring (optional – try using ground Annatto seeds)

2 free-range chicken breasts, skinned

For the flatbreads:

500g strong flour

10g salt

1 clove of garlic, thinly sliced

1 tsp cumin seeds, toasted

7g dried yeast

320ml warm water

To build the kebab:

Mixed lettuce leaves

Red cabbage, finely sliced

Carrot, grated

Pomegranate seeds

White onion, finely sliced

Wedge of lemon

Fresh coriander and mint

Method

For the tandoori kebab

Firstly toast the spices in a hot dry pan until lightly browned, and then pour them into a bowl. Mix in the yoghurt, ginger, lemon, garlic, salt and food colouring if using. Dice the chicken, mix with the spiced yoghurt and leave to marinate for 24 hours.

Skewer the chicken on a metal kebab skewer and cook under a hot grill for around 15 minutes, turning regularly but ensuring you get some good dark colour on the kebab.

For the flatbreads

Mix the flour, salt, garlic, and cumin seeds in a bowl. Dissolve the yeast in the warm water and combine with the dry ingredients. Bring the dough together, turn out onto a work surface and knead for a couple of minutes, then let it prove for 20 minutes. Once proved, divide the dough into four balls and roll out thinly on a floured surface to roughly 20cm rounds. Brush the flatbreads with oil and prick evenly with a fork. Leave for 10 minutes to prove a little, and then cook one at a time in a pan on a medium heat with a little oil until golden, charred and cooked through. They should take about 6 to 8 minutes.

To build the kebab

Place the warm flatbread on the plate. Top with a good handful of lettuce leaves, cabbage, grated carrot, pomegranate seeds and onion. Slide the tandoori kebab off the skewer on top of the filling, and finish with a good squeeze of lemon juice and a sprinkle of fresh coriander. Serve with more natural yoghurt mixed with fresh mint, and a good quality sweet chilli sauce if you like!

Going the
EXTRA MILE

Junction Bar's motto is Drinks:Social, which tells you exactly what the Chesterfield hotspot is all about and why it's been shortlisted for Bar of the Year – a title it currently holds from the previous year – in the 2018 Chesterfield Food and Drink Awards!

Junction Bar opened in November 2016 and quickly established itself as a hotspot for great drinks and great socialising at the start and end (depending on the time of night!) of Chesterfield's legendary Brampton Mile. Following extensive renovations to the venue, the bar now boasts a stylish but relaxed industrial interior thanks to cleverly used reclaimed materials. It's complemented by the extensive beer garden; the combination of deckchairs and an outdoor bar makes for an irresistible spot for sunny days.

Owner Michael Walker set up his first venture following a job as a flight attendant, so high standards of customer service are a given for him, and he based the menu of inventive as well as classic cocktails on his travels to various countries with work. There's also a collection of over 50 gins as well as wine, beers, real ale and premium lagers ready for the bar's busy evenings, especially Friday and Saturday nights when there's always a buzzing atmosphere. During the day there's food on the menu from Lambarelli's, the Italian takeaway just a couple of doors down, and generous helpings of coffee and spectacular cakes from a local supplier in Matlock.

Creating a friendly and welcoming vibe has been really important to Michael and his team, one of whom is especially good at encouraging customers to come and say hi… Olive the sausage dog is Junction Bar's official mascot and is always pleased to see four-legged friends popping by for a visit, where they too can have a cold drink and snaffle a treat from the bar! Events on bank holidays and other occasions draw lots of Michael's regular customers and new faces, and the line-up of artists for the lazy Sunday live music sessions is always one to look forward to.

Michael's still busy thinking up new ideas to keep his young venture moving forwards, with a plan to introduce pop-up street food on Saturdays in the pipeline…watch this space! Whether you're meeting friends for a casual afternoon catch up or enjoying a well-deserved cocktail or two at the end of the week, Junction Bar brings great drinks and great socialising together.

Junction Bar
PORNSTAR MARTINI

When designing the cocktail menu for Junction Bar, I wanted to include many of my favourites from all the fabulous destinations I visited during my time travelling as a first class air steward. The Pornstar Martini originated in Cape Town, and I would often enjoy one under the South African sunset. This cocktail is one of many on offer but has proved to be the most popular. Enjoy!

Preparation time: 5 minutes | Serves: 1

Ingredients

50ml premium vanilla vodka

25ml passoa

25ml passion fruit purée

25ml fresh orange juice

15ml sugar syrup

½ a passion fruit

1 tsp brown sugar

25ml prosecco

Method

Firstly, chill your martini glass with ice cubes.

Add the vodka, passoa, purée, orange juice, and sugar syrup to a Boston shaker glass. Add cubed ice and shake hard for 12-15 seconds. Empty the chilled martini glass and double strain the cocktail mixture into it.

Coat the cut side of the passion fruit half with brown sugar and blow torch until caramelised. Place onto a teaspoon and into the cocktail. Pour a shot of prosecco, and enjoy. Should I drink the prosecco or add it to the cocktail? The choice is yours!

Wined and DINED

A hand-picked selection of ales, wines and spirits with an all-inclusive menu of freshly cooked food: what more could you want from a traditional Derbyshire pub?

The Market Pub is owned and run by Douglas, who has been building its reputation for wine, whisky and ale alongside an ever-evolving menu of homemade food since 2007. Situated in Chesterfield's New Square, The Market is still a traditional pub but also keeps things fresh with a busy events calendar – such as gin, whisky or wine tastings – and new developments on the menu. The pub's selection of vegan options has been met with real enthusiasm and is now one of the largest in the area. Douglas is keen to continue expanding in this direction, saying "I find vegan food exciting to work with, and I do want to progress more so we can offer great food for everyone."

All of the creative dishes are brought to life in the kitchen by head chef Tracey and her team, who make everything fresh, from the pastry to the sauces, using quality ingredients including fresh seafood which is bought in every day. This and the legendary homemade pies are prominent features of the menu amidst a plethora of burgers, daily specials and main meals inspired by modern British and European cuisine from haggis to Bolognese. There's also a choose your own section, allowing meat-lovers, vegetarians and vegans alike to create their own plateful of fish, halloumi, falafel and much more with salads, sauces and sides all cooked with the love of great food that infuses The Market's whole menu.

Despite the array of food to choose from, matching a drink to your meal won't be a problem at The Market, as there's just as much emphasis on this aspect of the venture. Staff are trained so they can advise and help customers find their ideal tipple from an impressive selection of over 100 malt whiskies, 100 gins, 100 wines and over 300 ales! Douglas' own background is in wine, and he even used to pop into The Market for a drink when visiting his mum in the area before becoming its owner. It's important to him that the character of the Chesterfield pub isn't lost. "We want people to enjoy great food and great drinks in an informal setting," says Douglas, "so for me it's all about a relaxed atmosphere, and keeping things exciting as well as staying true to our ethos."

The Market Pub

FILLET OF ATLANTIC COD WITH MORCILLA BONBON AND ROMESCO SAUCE

The inspiration for this dish comes from many trips to beautiful Catalonia. We love the bold flavours and vibrant colours from this region, and looked to use wonderful, fresh ingredients to create this representative dish.

Preparation time: 40 minutes | Cooking time: 25 minutes | Serves: 4

Ingredients

For the Romesco sauce:

1 large roasted red pepper, skinned

2 cloves of garlic, smashed

170g slivered almonds, toasted

85g tomato purée

2 tbsp chopped flat-leaf parsley

2 tbsp sherry vinegar

1 tsp smoked paprika

½ tsp cayenne pepper

100ml extra-virgin olive oil

Fine sea salt and freshly ground black pepper

For the black olive, almond and parsley dressing:

50g black olives

15g flaked almonds

A few small flat leaf parsley leaves

Splash of Nunez de Prado olive oil

Splash of sherry vinegar

For the cod:

4 160g skin-on cod fillets

Olive oil and butter

For the charred leek:

2 medium-sized baby leeks

For the morcilla bonbon:

1 morcilla (blood sausage)

Plain flour

1 egg, beaten

200g Panko breadcrumbs

Fine sea salt and freshly ground black pepper

Method

For the Romesco sauce

Pulse the first eight ingredients in a food processor until very finely chopped. With the motor running, slowly add the oil and continue to process until smooth. Season with salt and pepper.

For the black olive, almond and parsley dressing

Finely chop the olives, almonds and parsley. Combine with the olive oil and vinegar and season to taste.

For the cod

Lightly coat the base of a non-stick frying pan with olive oil then place the pan over a medium-high heat. Once the pan is hot, season the cod with salt and place it in the pan skin-side down. Cook for 3-4 minutes until the skin is nicely golden and crisp. Turn over, add a knob of butter and transfer immediately to a hot oven for 4 minutes.

For the charred leek

Halve the leeks lengthways. Brush the leeks with oil and season with salt and pepper. Grill over a high heat until charred all over; about 3 minutes.

For the morcilla bonbon

Roll pieces of the morcilla to about the size of a walnut. Coat them in plain flour, then egg, then the breadcrumbs. Season with salt and pepper. Deep fry the bonbons until they are cooked through and the crumb coating is golden. Be sure the oil is not too hot or they will burn on the outside and be raw in the middle.

To serve

Remove the cod from the hot pan and season again. Arrange a line of the Romesco sauce on the plate and place the charred leek across it at an angle. Place the cod in the middle of the plate on top of the leek and spoon the dressing neatly around the edge. Add the bonbon and garnish with sliced olives, almonds and parsley leaves.

Two's COMPANY

Two award-winning ale houses nestled in the quaint Peak District hamlet of Whitehough, The Old Hall Inn and Paper Mill Inn offer food, drinks, and an atmosphere that's uniquely theirs.

A tiny hamlet, two pubs across the road from one another, and a family business: The Old Hall Inn and Paper Mill Inn are a unique combination of old and new. Managed by landlord Dan Capper, they have been developed by Dan and his family to incorporate food, drink, and accommodation that are full of character and great taste.

The Old Hall Inn was built as a coaching house, adjoining a manor house with medieval origins that was rebuilt in 1559, and in more recent times it was Dan's family home. The Paper Mill Inn started life as farm buildings which were converted into a tavern by a local landowner to provide a watering hole for his workers. Both have retained plenty of their distinctive features; the Paper Mill has a more industrial feel with exposed brick and beams lit by Edison bulbs, whereas the Old Hall beautifully mingles Elizabethan style and contemporary comfort to reflect its varied history.

Seasonal mains, pub classics and Derbyshire steaks all vie for attention on the mouth-watering menu based around the best produce Dan can find. All the lamb, for example, comes from one of the chef's farm and the pork doesn't have to travel far from its home in Edale. It's important to Dan that his team of chefs are allowed to be creative and have a lot of input when it comes to the recipes. "Everything is made fresh every day here – even accompaniments like sauces and pickles – so that we can make sure all our dishes from the steak and ale pudding to the confit duck get the time and attention they deserve."

The Old Hall has not lost the jovial atmosphere of a bustling bar – it's been awarded Derbyshire's CAMRA Pub of the Year multiple times – but it also welcomes everyone for lunch and evening meals or a proper Sunday roast in the restaurant that spills through the interconnected dining spaces. There's also a pub garden in front of The Old Hall, very popular for enjoying the Paper Mill's hand-stretched pizzas, and a terrace that's perfectly suited to a glass of wine in the sunshine. The business is a real marriage of two minds; as Dan puts it, "we are proud to be a traditional pub, as well as bringing something unique in terms of eating and drinking to the Peaks."

The Old Hall Inn
HUMMUS AND MOROCCAN SCOTCH EGG

Pete's lamb was in season when we were deciding on a recipe to put in this book, so we couldn't not use it. Our chef Luke drew on his recent travels for inspiration, but it's using the best local produce – lamb and farm-fresh eggs – that makes all the difference.

Preparation time: 25 minutes | Cooking time: approximately 20 minutes| Serves: 4

Ingredients

For the hummus:

2 tbsp tahini

100ml iced water

1 lemon, juiced

200g chickpeas

1 clove of garlic

1 tbsp cumin

3 tbsp olive oil

Salt and pepper to taste

For the Moroccan Scotch egg:

4 eggs

1 onion

3 cloves of garlic

2 tbsp cumin

1 tbsp paprika

1 tbsp chilli powder

Salt and pepper

160g minced lamb

Handful of coriander

Flour

Beaten egg

Japanese breadcrumbs

Olive oil

Method

For the hummus

Whip the tahini, water and lemon juice until it has a nice creamy texture. Place the mixture in a food processor with the chickpeas, garlic, cumin and olive oil then blitz until smooth. Add salt and pepper to taste.

For the Moroccan Scotch egg

Bring a pan of water to the boil and gently lower the eggs in. After 5 minutes of boiling, remove the eggs and put them in iced water to cool. Dice the onion and garlic and sweat off on a gentle heat in a pan with the cumin, paprika, chilli, salt and pepper. Leave it to cool and then mix with the lamb. Add the chopped coriander and mix by hand well.

Peel the boiled eggs. Roll around 40 grams of the spiced lamb into a ball and then flatten it. Place the boiled egg in the middle and fold the lamb around it. Repeat until all eggs are covered. Roll each of the Scotch eggs in flour, then dip in the beaten egg, then coat in breadcrumbs.

Carefully place each egg in a deep fat fryer on 160°c for 6 minutes or alternatively, in a pan filled with oil. Use a sugar thermometer to check the temperature of the pan if you have one.

To serve

Our hummus and Moroccan Scotch egg is best served with a good chilli jam on the side.

The Old Hall Inn
LAMB WELLINGTON

This is a firm favourite at our pub. We're lucky enough to have our very own King-Sterndale sheep farmer as one of our chefs, so we know that lamb's always on top form. The key to this dish is the quality of the ingredients so be sure to ask your butcher for advice when buying the meat. Created by chef Adam.

Preparation time: 25 minutes | Cooking time: 50 minutes | Serves: 4

Ingredients

1 chicken breast

Pinch of salt

1 clove of garlic

1 tbsp chopped parsley

1 tbsp chopped mint

2 eggs

300g butter

250ml cream

1 whole lamb loin

1 pack of ready-rolled pastry

1kg Rooster potatoes

1 egg, beaten

100ml milk

Vegetables, to finish

Method

Preheat the oven to 190°c before blitzing the chicken breast in a food processor with the salt, garlic, chopped parsley and mint. Add 1 egg, 50g butter and 50ml of cream. Blitz for a further minute.

Sear the lamb loin in a hot pan then take out and leave to cool. Unroll the pastry on a lightly floured surface. Add a thick layer of the chicken mousse while making sure to leave a gap around the edges so you can close it up. Place the lamb loin in the centre of the mousse and then wrap tightly, making sure there's no air inside, and fold each end up. Place in the fridge to rest for 20 minutes.

Peel and chop the potatoes. Place in a pan with salted water. Bring to the boil and simmer until cooked. Mash the potatoes and add the milk, the remaining cream and butter before placing it back on the stove, stirring occasionally.

Cover a baking tray with baking parchment paper and brush the top of the lamb wellington with beaten egg. Place in the oven for 14 minutes until golden brown. Turn the lamb wellington over and egg wash again. Cook for a further 5 minutes. Remove from the oven and leave to rest for at least 8 minutes before slicing.

To serve

Add whichever vegetables you would prefer to accompany the lamb wellington.

The Old Hall Inn

LADYBOWER TROUT, CRAYFISH BUTTER, WILD GARLIC JERSEY ROYALS

We love the earthy flavours of our locally caught trout, and we also enjoy seeing local produce traded for local beer... It always tastes better when you know the full story and you eat while sharing a beer or two! Created by chef Tom.

Preparation time: 20 minutes | Cooking time: 45 minutes | Serves: 4

Ingredients

1 whole trout, filleted, scaled and pinned

500g Jersey Royals

1 shallot, diced

1 clove of garlic, crushed

75g crayfish tails

100ml white wine

100g butter

1 lemon

Pinch of finely chopped tarragon

Knob of butter

Pinch of salt

1kg rainbow chard

Method

First boil the Jersey Royals in salted water for 20 minutes until tender, and then roast them in olive oil with the wild garlic leaves for 20 minutes.

To make the butter sauce, sauté the shallot, garlic, and crayfish together. Add the white wine and reduce by half, then whisk in the butter gradually so it emulsifies. Finish the sauce with a squeeze of lemon juice, some fresh tarragon and salt to taste.

To cook the trout, place skin side down in a pan on a medium heat and cook for 3 minutes. Flip the fish over and cook for 1 minute, then finish with butter and lemon juice.

To serve

Serve the pan fried trout and Jersey Royals with the butter sauce drizzled over and some rainbow chard boiled for a few minutes and then sautéed in butter.

The Old Hall Inn

PIZZA

Our pizza is made to a very authentic Italian recipe using olive oil and the double rising method. The quality of the flour is also very important and '00' is the best grade. This is great fun to make with the kids and perfect for experimenting with different toppings.

Preparation time: 30 minutes | Cooking time: 30 minutes | Serves: 4

Ingredients

For the pizza dough:

320ml tap water, at room temperature

2g dried yeast

Pinch of salt

600g pizza flour (00)

20g semolina

Olive oil, to finish

For the tomato sauce:

Splash of olive oil

1 white onion

1 clove of garlic, finely chopped

1 glass of red wine

Slug of red wine vinegar

1 tin of good quality chopped tomatoes

1 tbsp tomato purée

1 tsp brown sugar

A few basil leaves

Salt and pepper, to taste

Method

For the pizza dough

Add the water and yeast to the mixer or bowl and mix until well combined and the water is cloudy with no lumps. Add the salt, half of the flour and all the semolina. Mix until you get a smooth paste, then add the rest of the flour until the mix is firm and dry to touch. Gradually add olive oil to the dough until the oil is fully accepted into the mixture and gives the dough a glossy sheen. Place the finished dough onto a well-floured surface, cover with cling film and leave to prove for 20 minutes.

When the dough has risen slightly divide into four equal parts, shape each part into a ball and leave on the worktop for the dough to prove again until it's ready to roll out to the ideal size and thickness for your preference. This could take 20 minutes to 1 hour, as it needs to double in size.

For the tomato sauce

Heat the olive oil in a pan and finely dice the onion. Cook the onion in olive oil until soft (about 4-5 minutes on a medium heat). Add the garlic and cook for further minute. Add the red wine and the red wine vinegar. Cook until the liquid has reduced by half and all the alcohol has evaporated. Add the chopped tomato, purée and sugar and simmer for 1 hour on a low heat until mixture has reduced to a thicker sauce consistency. Add water if too thick. Add salt, pepper and basil to taste. Blend the sauce in a food processor or using a hand blender to purée it. Leave to cool and apply to pizza bases using a ladle to add a thin layer of sauce.

To cook

Add whatever toppings you like; just one tip though: less is more, in both number and quantity. If using a cured Parma ham or similar ingredient, add immediately after the pizza comes out of the oven. There will be enough heat in the pizza itself to gently cook the ham without spoiling it. Get the oven as hot as possible and cook the pizza for 10 minutes or until the base is golden and the cheese is bubbling (it takes us around 3 minutes in a 280°c oven).

The Old Hall Inn

DERBYSHIRE RASPBERRY AND CHOCOLATE TART WITH FOREST GIN AND TONIC SORBET

Seeing as we enjoy drinking our local Forest Gin so much, we figured we'd enjoy eating it in equal measure. The intensity of the gin sorbet is refreshing and works incredibly with the sweet tart and the flavour of our local raspberries. Created by chef Ben.

Preparation time: 30 minutes, plus chilling time | Cooking time: 1 hour | Serves: 8-10

Ingredients

For the raspberry and chocolate tart:

500g plain flour

180g unsalted butter

175g icing sugar

2 lemons, juiced

5 eggs

150g unsalted butter

225g dark chocolate

2 egg yolks

45g caster sugar

Drop of vanilla essence

Wild raspberries

For the forest gin and tonic sorbet:

250ml water

250g caster sugar

8 tbsp Forest Gin (or your own favourite gin)

375ml tonic water

1 lemon, juiced

1 egg white

Method

For the raspberry and chocolate tart

To make the sweet pastry, rub the flour, butter and icing sugar together in a bowl until it forms a crumb texture. Mix the lemon juice with three eggs and add it to the crumbs. Mix until it becomes dough, then cling film and refrigerate. After 2 hours remove the mixture from the fridge and let it come up to room temperature.

Roll out the pastry and place into a baking tin before refrigerating for 30 minutes. Place the pastry in the oven at 150°c and blind bake for 20 minutes. Remove the baking beans and seal the pastry by brushing with an egg yolk. Bake for a further 5 minutes and then take out of the oven to cool.

To make the filling, melt the butter and chocolate together. Whisk together the remaining whole eggs, two egg yolks, caster sugar and vanilla essence until the mixture is at ribbon stage. Fold the melted chocolate and egg mixture together.

Add the raspberries to the tart case before pouring in the filling. Bake at 120°c for around 20 minutes. Remove from oven and leave the tart to cool for around 2 hours.

For the forest gin and tonic sorbet

Stir 250ml water and 250g caster sugar together before simmering until the sugar dissolves and then leaving to chill. Mix the gin, tonic, and lemon juice with the sugar syrup in a bowl and then place it in the freezer, but continue to stir every 5 minutes till the mixture is slushy. Whisk an egg white until it becomes light and fluffy and stir it into the gin and tonic mixture. Leave the sorbet to freeze overnight.

To serve

The gin and tonic sorbet and raspberry chocolate tart make a perfect combination and are best served together.

Lunch on THE HOOF

Tradition, character, history and comfort meet at The Packhorse Inn, a quintessential English country pub surrounded by some of the most striking scenery in the Peak District.

The Packhorse Inn has served as a watering hole for locals and travellers alike since 1787. Formerly two miners' cottages, it lies on an old packhorse route running from Chesterfield through Baslow to Little Longstone, before climbing up towards Peak District beauty spot Monsal Head.

The inn is perfectly situated for those enjoying a day out rambling in the nearby countryside, cycling the Monsal Trail, or visiting a range of nearby attractions including Chatsworth House and Haddon Hall. It's a cosy retreat in the winter too thanks to comfortable furnishings and a roaring log fire.

Boasting an acknowledgement in the 2018 Good Beer Guide, the Packhorse is also a haven for beer lovers after a "good honest pint". The bar often features Black Sheep, award-winning cask ales from the Thornbridge Brewery, and hand pulls for a regularly changing cider and guest beer. There's also a concise but effective selection of wines, provided by Hattersley Wines in Bakewell, and a full range of spirits to wet your whistle whatever tipple you fancy after a day fly fishing or walking in the Peaks.

Visitors can also settle in a snug corner and tuck into fresh, local food. The daily changing blackboard menu features local game and meat from Bakewell's finest butchers. "As most people in Derbyshire can't walk 50 feet without encountering a cow, a pig, or a sheep, we didn't think it made a lot of sense to get them from anywhere else," is the team's ethos. There's even a quirky 'tapas' menu featuring beef dripping and pork pie.

Sticking to a theme, cheeses come from the Hartington Cheese Shop while bread and Bakewell pudding is lovingly baked at the Original Bakewell Pudding Shop.

Good food is served every day, beer flows plentifully and there's an ever-popular Thursday night quiz throughout the year which raises plenty of laughs as well as thousands of pounds for charity. What more could you want from an English country pub?

The Packhorse Inn
ONGLET STEAK WITH MUSHROOM AND RED WINE SAUCE, POMME PURÉE AND GREENS

More commonly known in English as Hanger Steak or butcher's trim, this coarse-grained cut of beef comes from the diaphragm and is packed full of flavour, making it a great pub steak. The meat should be hung for a minimum of 21 days, longer if possible and cooked no more than medium rare. Always slice it thinly and across the grain.

Preparation time: 15 minutes, plus resting time | Cooking time: approx. 45 minutes | Serves: 4

Ingredients

4 6–8oz onglet steaks

Splash of oil

For the pomme purée:

750g potatoes (such as Maris Piper)

150ml full fat milk, heated

60g butter, cut into cubes

3 tbsp double cream

Salt and pepper, to taste

For the mushroom and red wine sauce:

6 shallots

2 cloves of garlic

110g butter

450g chestnut mushrooms

300ml red wine

Sprigs of thyme

Method

For the pomme purée

Peel and cut the potatoes into evenly sized pieces and boil in salted water for 12-15 minutes until soft. Drain and press the potatoes through a mouli or potato ricer until completely lump free. Heat the milk in a separate saucepan. Put the potatoes back in the pan and whisk in half the butter and double cream. Slowly add the warmed milk and continue whisking until it becomes a velvety purée. Add more of the butter if necessary. Season to taste and set aside.

For the mushroom and red wine sauce

Dice the shallots and garlic and fry in butter until soft. Quarter the mushrooms, add to the pan and cook until browned. Add the red wine and allow to reduce by half. Add thyme leaves and salt and pepper to taste.

To serve

Heat a large frying pan and add a little oil. Cook the steaks for no more than 3-4 minutes on each side until rare to medium rare. Allow to rest in a warm place for 10-15 minutes and season while resting. Slice thinly across the grain and pour the sauce over half the steak, then plate up with the pomme purée and your chosen greens. Tuck in!

Shake a tail
FEATHER

Fifteen individually styled rooms and the very best local produce cooked by Michelin-trained chefs and served in an atmospheric restaurant and bar: The Peacock at Rowsley has everything you could want for a day or a stay on the Haddon Estate in the Peak District.

Like its namesake, The Peacock at Rowsley has plenty to show off about, but the intentions for this boutique hotel are to provide comfort, good food, and originality without the preening. Lord and Lady Edward Manners are the owners of the former manor house, which had been in the family for centuries until it was sold during the 1950s. They always regretted the loss, though, so it was fortunate that Edward was able to bring it back into the fold when he bought The Peacock in 2001. Hospitality runs in his family, evident in the style and attention to detail that has given The Peacock such warmth and welcome.

Although the restaurant tends towards fine dining, locals and visitors – whether staying for a week or popping by for Sunday lunch – are encouraged to feel relaxed and simply enjoy the surroundings alongside the seasonal menus. Head chef Dan Smith, who has been at The Peacock since 2007, describes the food as "classically rooted but with a modern approach" and above all driven by the ingredients around them. Good relationships with suppliers are vital, he explains, such as their butcher in Darley Dale who sources beef for The Peacock

from Bakewell Cattle Market. You won't see asparagus in October or strawberries in February on your plate at The Peacock, but good honest food that's original without being pretentious is always in abundance.

The bar has a menu too – with favourites like steak and chips alongside pints of local beer – to enjoy amidst warm lighting on polished wood, stone, and cosy furnishing. The Peacock is a perfect marriage of its beautiful countryside setting and a spot of luxury; opportunities abound for walking and fishing on the Haddon estate, and its proximity to both Haddon Hall and Chatsworth makes it a great base for those visiting the Peak District.

"We want to make this place very approachable and welcoming," says Lord Edward, "so people can enjoy a walk with their dog and have a sophisticated meal out afterwards." The Peacock's team has been curated with this in mind; the high quality of service stems from, in many cases, a longstanding commitment to the hotel and restaurant which they are rightly very proud to be a part of.

The Peacock at Rowsley

PIG'S HEAD CROQUETTES, CELERIAC, HAM AND TRUFFLE

A delicious starter that uses what is – in my opinion – an underrated part of the pig. Because of the fat to meat ratio, the meat remains moist and is packed full of flavour. Salt-baking the celeriac intensifies the flavour too. The dish could be served without the truffle if it's hard to get hold of.

Preparation time: approx. 10 hours | Cooking time: approx. 15 minutes | Serves: 10

Ingredients

For the pig's head croquettes:

½ a pig's head, split down the middle

250g onions

100g leeks

75g celery

200g carrots

7g thyme

2 bay leaves

50g gherkins

30g capers

3g parsley

25g flour

60g eggs, whisked together

125g breadcrumbs (panko if available)

For the salt-baked celeriac:

600g course sea salt

600g egg whites

1kg flour

1 celeriac

200ml whipping cream

To serve:

Cooked ham

Raw sliced celeriac

Lemon juice

Rapeseed oil

Truffle

Method

For the pig's head croquettes

Peel and roughly chop the onions, carrots, celery and leeks. Place into a large pan with a little oil and colour until golden brown. Add the pig's head, thyme, garlic and bay leaves, and cover with cold water. Bring to a boil and turn down to a gentle simmer. Braise the pig's head on a low heat until the meat falls from the bone (this will take about 4 hours). Carefully lift the braised pig's head out of the stock and allow it to cool enough to handle. Using a spoon, carefully remove the skin and discard. Place all the cooked meat into a bowl and gently flake up. Add the chopped gherkin, capers and parsley to the flaked meat and mix together with a little salt. Pack the mixture into a terrine mould or a plastic tub and set in the fridge overnight.

The next day, turn out the meat and cut into cubes. Dip into flour, then the whisked eggs and then the breadcrumbs. Store in the fridge until needed.

For the salt-baked celeriac

Mix together the salt, egg whites and flour to form a dough, encase the celeriac in it and bake in the oven at 180°c until cooked through (this should take about 1 hour 30 minutes). Take out of the oven and allow to cool. When cooled, break open the dough and remove the celeriac. Using a knife, peel the skin from the celeriac and discard. Cut the baked celeriac into cubes the same size as the pig's head croquettes and reserve all the trim.

Place the celeriac trim in a pan and cover halfway with cream. Bring up to a boil and reduce by half, then place in a blender and blend until smooth.

To serve

Deep fry the pig's head croquettes in a fryer at 180°c until the breadcrumbs are golden. Warm the celeriac cubes in a little water and butter, and add the cooked ham. Warm the purée. Serve with thinly sliced raw celeriac dressed in a little lemon juice, salt and rapeseed oil. Grate truffle over the plate if using to finish.

The Peacock at Rowsley

BEEF FILLET AND CHEEK, ARTICHOKES, MISO HOLLANDAISE

We are lucky to have the most amazing Derbyshire beef on our doorstep. This recipe showcases two different cuts of meat. At The Peacock, we cook our own baby globe artichokes, but you can buy cooked ones from a good deli for a home version of this recipe.

Preparation time: approx. 6 hours | Cooking time: approximately 20 minutes | Serves: 4

Ingredients

For the ox cheek:

1 ox cheek

500ml red wine

130g onions, roughly chopped

70g each of carrots and celery, roughly chopped

2 cloves of garlic

10g thyme

1 bay leaf

700ml brown chicken stock

For the Jerusalem artichoke discs and crisps:

500g Jerusalem artichokes

50ml lemon juice

3g salt

250g butter

For the miso hollandaise:

45ml white wine vinegar

4 peppercorns

1 bay leaf

2 egg yolks

10g white miso paste

125g clarified butter

Lemon juice, to taste

To serve:

4 140g beef fillet portions

Knob of butter

1 hispi cabbage

20g each of baby watercress, chives and shallots

4 cooked baby globe artichokes, cut in half lengthways

Method

For the ox cheek

Trim the ox cheek and place in a tub with the red wine, vegetables and herbs. Refrigerate overnight. The next day, strain and reserve the wine. Colour the ox cheek in a hot pan with a little oil until golden brown all over. Remove from the pan, add a little more oil and cook the vegetables and herbs until golden brown, then add the red wine and reduce by two thirds. Add the chicken stock and bring to the boil. Place the ox cheek back into the pan, cover with greaseproof paper and gently simmer until the cheek is tender (about 4 hours). When the ox cheek is cooked, carefully remove from the pan, leave to cool and then place in the fridge until completely cold. Strain the cooking stock and reduce down to sauce consistency, skimming off any impurities.

For the Jerusalem artichoke discs and crisps

For the discs, peel and slice 400g of the artichokes into 20 discs using a cutter. Combine 500ml of water with the lemon juice, salt and butter in a pan and bring to the boil. Add the artichoke discs and cook until tender. For the crisps, peel the remaining artichokes and slice thinly on a Japanese mandoline, then deep fry at 165°c until golden. Drain on kitchen paper and season with salt.

For the miso hollandaise

Bring the vinegar to the boil with the peppercorns and bay leaf; reduce by two thirds then strain. Place the reduction into a metal bowl with the miso paste, egg yolks, and a little hot water. Whisk over a bain-marie until the eggs are cooked to a sabayon, then slowly whisk in the clarified butter, season with salt and lemon juice and pass through a fine sieve.

To serve

To cook the fillet, season with salt and sear in a hot pan until golden brown all over. Add a knob of butter to the pan, baste the beef and then place into a preheated oven at 180°c until cooked to your liking. Remove from the pan and rest in a warm place for 5-10 minutes, then half each portion.

Shred the hispi cabbage and blanch in boiling water. Drain, add butter and season. Roast the baby artichokes in a pan with a little oil, add the Jerusalem artichoke discs and a knob of butter, baste until golden and drain. Portion the ox cheek into four and warm in the red wine sauce.

Place a mound of the cabbage on the plate and place the fillet on top. Pour some of the reduced stock from the cheek over. Place the ox cheek next to it, cover with the hollandaise and sprinkle with finely chopped shallots and chives. Place the vegetables neatly onto the plate and garnish with the artichoke crisps and watercress.

Peak PROVENANCE

From producers to private dining, Peak District Deli is all about celebrating one of the most beautiful areas in the UK by showcasing its fantastic food and drink.

Ralph and Lauren Wilson began their venture in 2017, with a concept for a business based in the area they both love that provides a platform for its most skilled food and drink producers. Peak District Deli gives you a wide selection of products, all of which have been created in the Peaks, brought together in the form of an online shop with collections from preserves to poultry. The food and drink you pick will be delivered to your door the following Friday or Saturday; their commitment to running an environmentally friendly business means that efficiency is really important, as well as using recyclable packaging and donating any excess products to the High Peak Food Bank and other local projects.

Along the same lines, reducing food miles is part of the reason Ralph and Lauren only work with Peak District producers, whether they're making bean to bar chocolate or blue cheese. Ethical and sustainable sourcing forms the backbone of Ralph and Lauren's business, so forming good relationships with suppliers is something they've put time and effort into, along with making sure their welfare standards match up. "Our producers all have a story to tell, and on our part it's great to be able to provide a shop window for them which

they wouldn't necessarily have otherwise," Ralph says. The couple are hoping to continue expanding the deli, conscious that interest in provenance is only increasing when it comes to food.

The other aspects of Ralph and Lauren's venture follow exactly the same train of thought; private dining, event catering, and pop-up dinners are regular features of their eclectic calendar. Lauren, a chef by trade, creates menus bespoke to the individual or group they're working with. Her influences come from all over the world, but particularly Spain and India where she lived and worked before moving to Ralph's home county. The pop-up dinners are created in collaboration with producers, and all the catering uses the same wonderful food and drink sold in the deli.

The convenience of online shopping, or being catered for, is married with a deep commitment to great quality food and drink that's completely traceable and made locally at Peak District Deli. Lauren and Ralph hope to show their customers just how wonderful the skilled, passionate and dedicated producers around them are while protecting, preserving and supporting the incredible landscape they work in.

Peak District Deli

BARBECUED DERBYSHIRE LEG OF LAMB WITH GARDEN HERB SALSA VERDE

The perfect sharing recipe for a family feast or an alfresco dinner party. With smoky locally reared lamb and fresh garden herb salsa verde as the stars, this is packed full of flavour. Many of the ingredients in the recipe are available to buy through our online shop and we deliver at your chosen timeslot too. This recipe supports small independent producers, farmers and charities in the Peak District.

Preparation time: 10 minutes, plus 1 hour 30 minutes resting | Cooking time: 1-5 hours | Serves: 8

Ingredients

For the salsa verde:

4-5 anchovies in oil, drained

3 cloves of garlic, peeled

2 tbsp Dijon mustard

1 lemon, juiced

Large bunch of picked rosemary leaves

Large bunch of parsley

Large bunch of mint

Large handful of thyme leaves

2 tbsp apple cider vinegar

2 tbsp rapeseed oil

10g sea salt

Pinch of black pepper, freshly ground

For the lamb:

4kg bone-in leg of locally reared lamb

Method

For the salsa verde

Add all the ingredients into a food processor. Blitz to a rough paste, adding more oil if it is too thick. Adjust the seasoning to your liking.

For the lamb

Make deep, diagonal slashes along the top of the lamb leg and put it in a roasting tin. Massage half of the salsa verde all over the lamb, getting it into all the cuts. Leave the lamb for 1 hour or so to come up to room temperature and put the other half of the salsa verde aside for serving.

Set up your barbecue for two-zone cooking (coals only on one side of the barbecue) with the hotter, direct side at a medium heat (around 160°c). Put the lamb on the hot side of the barbecue and cook for 15 minutes, turning every 2-3 minutes until the meat is seared and browned all over. Then move the lamb over to the cooler, indirect side of the barbecue to cook through.

At this point, decide if you're going to roast the lamb hot and fast or low and slow. For hot and fast, keep the temperature at around 160°c and cook the lamb with the lid on the barbecue for a further 45 minutes, or until the internal temperature hits 65°c, at which point the lamb will be pink and juicy.

For low and slow, put the lid on the barbecue and clamp down the vents at the bottom of the barbecue until the temperature stabilises at around 120°c. Cook the lamb until the internal temperature hits around 90°c (about 5 hours) by which point it will shred beautifully.

Remove the lamb from the barbecue. Cover loosely with foil and leave to rest for 30 minutes.

Alternatively, you could sear the lamb on the barbecue and finish it off in the oven covered in foil at 120°c for 4-5 hours. Check it's not too dry, and if so just add a splash of water to the roasting tin.

To serve

Slice or pull the lamb and serve with the remaining salsa verde drizzled over the top.

The lamb goes especially well with an oriental leaf salad, cucumber tzatziki, roast beetroot, crumbled feta, balsamic vinegar and flatbreads. Serve on large wooden boards and sharing platters, making the food a real feature of your dinner party or occasion.

Home away from HOME

The approach of Rowley's Village Pub in Baslow is a unique one these days... A pub in the heart of Derbyshire that revolves around local produce, great food and a real sense of community!

The collaboration between Max and Susan Fischer, who established the country house hotel Fischer's Baslow Hall and Rupert Rowley, their head chef turned out to be fruitful in more ways than one. In 2006 the pub in the village of Baslow underwent a complete redevelopment to become Rowley's Village Pub and Restaurant. It began with a simplified and honest approach to food that made seasonal and local produce the centre of attention. Rowley's Village Pub has become a successful part of the local community as it continues to move with the times and keep things consistent and interesting.

Head chef Adam Harper, a local lad, changes the menu according to the time of year and features traditional favourites like fish and chips as well as inventive modern British fare. Adam has worked alongside Rupert as sous chef after starting with Fischer's at the age of 17. He now looks to wow diners in a different way at Rowley's; using flavour and an emphasis on bringing fresh, local produce to the table is the keystone to his success.

Rowley's is a village pub like no other in the area. The team marry a sense of community with a top end proper pub, led by Tom Schofield, himself born and bred in Derbyshire. Tom carries an energy that empowers the team. "It's not just great fresh food and fun service, but a genuine experience for our customers whether local or strangers," he says.

With three contemporary dining areas, a bar serving unique and interesting wines and hand-crafted ales, and a welcome that extends to muddy boots, mucky paws and wet anoraks, it's the perfect mix. Informal but well looked after, Rowley's is the local that reminds us of what pubs used to be: a home away from home.

Rowley's Village Pub
CARAMELISED WHITE CHOCOLATE AND STRAWBERRY ICE CREAM SANDWICH

This recipe is a twist on one of my childhood favourites and is one of the biggest sellers at Rowley's, especially during the hot summer days.

Preparation time: 50 minutes, plus overnight | Cooking time: 1 hour 30 minutes | Serves: 8-10

Ingredients

For the strawberry parfait:

500g strawberry purée

1 lemon, juiced

150g sugar

100g MSK ice cream stabilizer

400g whipping cream

For the lemon jelly:

3 leaves of bronze leaf gelatine

300ml lemon juice

100ml sugar syrup

For the strawberry sorbet:

500g strawberry purée

350ml water

150g sugar

1 lemon, juiced

50g MSK ice cream stabilizer

For the strawberry and mint purée:

500g fresh English strawberries

1 lemon, zested and juiced

75g sugar

25g fresh mint

1 drop of garden mint flavouring

For the caramelised white chocolate:

300g white chocolate

For the lemon curd:

3 eggs

3 egg yolks

270g sugar

3 lemons, zested and juiced

150g butter

To serve:

150g fresh strawberries

Method

For the strawberry parfait

Heat the strawberry purée, lemon juice, sugar and ice cream stabilizer to 750°c and then chill in the fridge. Whip the cream, and when the strawberry mix is cold fold in the whipped cream. Line a deep baking tray with baking parchment, carefully pour the mixture into the tray and freeze overnight. Once frozen stamp out into discs.

For the lemon jelly

Soak the gelatine in ice cold water. Boil the lemon juice and sugar syrup together then add the gelatine. Pour the mixture into a flat-bottomed tub and refrigerate overnight.

For the strawberry sorbet

Boil all the ingredients together then transfer to a bowl and cool in the fridge. Churn the sorbet in an ice cream machine or stir every half hour while it's freezing.

For the strawberry and mint purée

Mix all the ingredients together in a blender and then pass through a chinois or fine sieve. Put into a piping bag.

For the caramelised white chocolate

Line a baking tray with baking parchment. Melt the chocolate and spread it out on the tray. Bake the chocolate at 170°c for 8 minutes. When it comes out of the oven, cut the chocolate into discs the same size as the parfait straight away. Let it set, then peel off the tray.

For the lemon curd

Combine the eggs, yolks, sugar, lemon juice and zest in a pan. Cook on a gentle heat until the mixture coats the back of a spoon. Once cooked, slowly add the butter and stir until emulsified.

To serve

Place a white chocolate disc in the centre of the plate. Place one of the strawberry parfait discs on top, then finish with another white chocolate disc and that's your ice cream sandwich. Slice the fresh strawberries and fan out around the ice cream sandwich. With the lemon curd and strawberry mint purée, pipe random dots around the plate. Using a little spoon, scoop out pieces of the lemon jelly and place them on and around the ice cream sandwich. Finish with a scoop of strawberry sorbet on top of the ice cream sandwich.

Italy in A JAR

With a little help from Puglia tomatoes, Teresa Lambarelli built a little Italy in the heart of Chesterfield, based on tradition, honesty, and over 40 years of experience.

Ever since Teresa Lambarelli was a little girl, pasta sauce has been flowing through her veins. Working with her Italian father in his pizza takeaway business – the first in Chesterfield and still there to this day – she mastered the classic recipes and contributed to the excellence the family-run eatery was known for.

When Teresa's father was finally ready to pass the baton, life got in the way and she had to leave the restaurant. Moving onto working at a school kitchen, she realised how far removed the wholesale sauces were from the natural, wholesome ingredients she knew and loved. Pimped with additives, artificial flavours and heaps of sugar, they sparked an idea for producing her own healthy, gimmick-free alternatives.

The home manufacturing business soon kicked off, as jars of Teresa's pasta sauce received fantastic responses at farmer's markets; those cherished the most came from fellow Italians, who claimed it tasted "better than Nonna's back home". As soon as the demand grew further than a domestic kitchen could take, her family restaurant made their premises available for Teresa to do her magic.

In 2011, Teresa renamed the traditional family venue to Teresa Lambarelli's Italian Caffè and Pasta Bar, selling the developed range of sauces, dressings and biscotti, as well as serving authentic Italian dishes, some named after Teresa's daughters! With plum tomatoes imported from South Italy as the primary ingredient, Teresa's authentic sauces have conquered hearts and stomachs both locally and internationally, equally appreciated by Derbyshire school kids and Italian distributors.

Although the products preserve tradition, a lot has changed in the restaurant's décor. The national colours of green, white and red have been replaced with more contemporary blues and greys, with archways paying homage to Mediterranean trattorias. The café downstairs, next door to the original pizza takeaway now owned by Teresa's sister, serves delicious Portioli coffee sourced from Milan and lunchtime paninis, while the upstairs restaurant opens on Saturday nights for set menu dining experiences. Evening specials also include 'Pasta and prosecco' nights with live music, where Teresa's delicacies can really sing.

Having won Chesterfield Food Producer of the Year three times, the business can boast a loyal clientele, fully booked Saturdays, and a dedicated team. Teresa's story proves that success can always be stored away for later; you just need that perfect moment to unscrew the lid.

Teresa Lambarelli's
LINGUINE DI MARE

My linguini di mare was inspired by di Vieste Puglia, near to my family's home town in Southern Italy where Italians feast on fresh seafood pasta dishes. This mouth-watering dish reflects just that, and linguini di mare brings a healthy and sophisticated twist to any family table.

Preparation time: 25 minutes | Cooking time: 15 minutes | Serves 2

Ingredients

2 tbsp butter

1 clove of garlic, minced

3 shallots, thinly sliced

1 tsp dried oregano

2 tsp freshly chopped dill, plus extra to garnish

6 tbsp dry white wine

300g mixed seafood (cockles, mussels, prawns, squid rings and tentacles)

2 tbsp fresh double cream

10 whole fresh cherry tomatoes

2 tsp fresh lemon juice

200g dried linguini pasta

Freshly grated Parmesan

Salt and pepper, to taste

Method

Bring a large pan of salted water to the boil. Meanwhile, melt the butter in a large frying pan over a medium heat. Add the garlic, shallots, oregano and a little of the dill and cook, stirring occasionally, for about 2 minutes. Add half of the white wine and reduce, then add the mixed seafood. Cook gently for 2 minutes, stirring occasionally. Add the cream, the rest of the white wine and the fresh tomatoes and increase the heat to medium-high. Simmer until the sauce has slightly thickened; about 2-3 minutes. Stir in the lemon juice. Add the pasta to the pan of boiling water and cook according to the directions on the package. Drain the pasta and transfer to the pan with the sauce. Stir to coat the pasta in the sauce and stir in the Parmesan. Season to taste with salt and pepper.

To serve

Serve immediately, topped with more Parmesan and a sprinkle of fresh dill.

Fresh is BEST

The White Horse at Woolley Moor is all about contemporary luxury and a fresh take on local produce; its driven and creative team are always bringing new ideas into the mix from Derbyshire and beyond.

David and Melanie are the husband and wife team behind one of Derbyshire's top end country pubs, The White Horse at Woolley Moor. In a little village surrounded by rolling hills, the owners and their team are proud to offer food and accommodation that reflects the attention to detail and high aspirations that have driven everything they've achieved since taking on the pub in 2007. The oldest parts of The White Horse can boast two centuries of history, but David and Melanie have married this with a modern approach to luxury in the rooms, which all have a balcony making the most of some beautiful views across the countryside, and on the menus.

Great food and a well-stocked bar are as integral to The White Horse as the warm and friendly atmosphere. David describes the food as "an eclectic mix that's hard to class" but what does tie it all together is fresh produce from the area. Head chef Craig Peters and his sous chef Jack work with a nearby dairy and butcher, amongst other suppliers, to source seasonal ingredients. This enables them to make everything

– even butter and ice cream – from scratch. "We start from the beginning in making our food whether it's a special, a real classic, or a new invention, and that's the key to it all," says David. Influences from Europe and Asia find their way into dishes made with Derbyshire's finest meat and vegetables, and the team are always on the lookout for new ideas and flavours to work on together.

Breakfast through to dinner can be enjoyed by a log fire in the winter or in outdoor seating over summer, and there's always a choice of three cask ales plus plenty of choice at the bar to wash it all down with. The beers rarely come from more than 15 miles away, explains David, who himself grew up just a few miles from The White Horse. The venture isn't just about running a country pub for him and Melanie; their aim is to provide something really special across the whole package of food, drink, rooms, and atmosphere. "We can say, hand on heart, that everything here is hand-picked," says David, "and you could choose anything from our menu because we're really proud of it all."

The White Horse at Woolley Moor

The White Horse at Woolley Moor

PAN ROASTED HALIBUT WITH A SAMPHIRE, ASPARAGUS AND SUGAR SNAP PEA RISOTTO

This halibut dish is a great example of one of our fish specials at The White Horse. The keys to the dish are to use as fresh as possible vegetables, good quality Parmesan and to have a tasty fish stock to bring depth of flavour through the risotto. If you can't source halibut, it can be replaced with another thick white fish such as cod, hake or monkfish.

Preparation time: 10 minutes | Cooking time: 25 minutes | Serves: 2

Ingredients

50g shallots, peeled and chopped

2 cloves of garlic, peeled and chopped

Olive oil

150g Arborio rice

100ml white wine

400ml fish stock

2 portions of halibut (170g-200g each)

Salt and pepper

6 asparagus spears, trimmed and chopped

40g samphire

40g sugar snap peas, sliced lengthwise

50g butter, diced

50g Parmesan, freshly grated

15g chives, chopped

To serve:

Garden herbs (any soft herbs such as parsley, bronze fennel, chives or winter savoury)

1 lemon

Method

Sweat the shallots and garlic in a little olive oil until they are soft but have no colour. Once the shallots are soft, add the rice and sweat for 1 minute. Add all of the white wine, bring to the boil, and cook while stirring constantly until almost all the wine has been absorbed. Gradually add the fish stock one ladle at a time, constantly keeping the rice moving in the pan.

While the rice is cooking, heat a non-stick pan with a little olive oil. Season the fish with salt and pepper. Place the fish in the pan and cook on one side for 2-3 minutes. Turn the fish over and cook for another 2-3 minutes. Turn once more, remove the pan from the heat and leave the fish in the pan to finish cooking. Cooking times vary depending on the thickness of the fish, so keep checking it while you finish the rest of the dish.

By this time the rice should almost be done. It should be tender with a slight bite, not chalky or overly soft. The liquid should be thick and creamy. Once the rice is cooked, add the asparagus, samphire, and sugar snaps. Stir for 1 minute then add the butter and Parmesan. Gently stir until the butter and cheese has melted and the risotto has a rich creamy consistency. At this point, taste the risotto and then add salt and pepper to your own taste. When you're happy with the flavour and consistency, add the chopped chives.

To serve

Serve the risotto in a large bowl and place the fish on top. Garnish with garden herbs and some wedges of fresh lemon.

Deliciously
DERBYSHIRE

Chris Mapp transformed a run-down village pub into a Derbyshire destination, now renowned for top quality food celebrating the best of the surrounding countryside.

The Tickled Trout is a proudly independent pub that sources the best Derbyshire produce owner and head chef Chris Mapp can find and transforms it into modern British food to tickle your tastebuds. Its light, airy dining area and relaxed lounge are the end result of a full renovation and Chris' vision for the high-end pub restaurant. Anyone is welcome at The Tickled Trout, whether for a sup of good ale, from his family's Collyfobble Brewery just down the road, or a full-blown Sunday lunch. Chris' ethos revolves around keeping things as local as possible; maintaining great relationships with suppliers like Jon at the Wye Bakehouse, Jane at Bradwell's Ice Cream and David at Highfield House Farm is crucial, alongside working with Adam from Country Fresh Foods on a seasonal basis.

With so much great produce to work with, including organic fresh fruit and veg from his mum's walled garden, Chris likes to keep things simple when it comes to showcasing flavours, especially from the more overlooked cuts of meat and fresh fish he likes to work with. Braised shoulder of beef, pork rib-eye, Cornish cod cheeks...the ingredients are the star of the show at The Tickled Trout, cooked with precision and passion. Sous chef Jack Butler and front of house managers Martyna Balinska and Francesca Payton are integral to the top-end execution of the dining experience, as well as the rest of the award-winning team Chris has brought together. He's confident enough in what they create at The Tickled Trout to know that they don't need to chase accolades; instead they focus on doing what they all do best.

Having come from the kitchens of Marcus Wareing and Gordon Ramsay, Chris has poured plenty of knowledge and talent into The Tickled Trout. He also cites his good friend Paul Ainsworth, with whom he co-owned a restaurant in Padstow, Cornwall, as a big influence on his cooking and says that running a pub is "in the DNA" thanks to his mum and dad. Chris grew up just outside Barlow, and learnt a lot from his dad's background in the industry. The Tickled Trout celebrates the marriage of all this; Derbyshire roots, the tradition of the great village pub, ingredients grown or reared in neighbouring fields, and above all, delicious food and drink.

The Tickled Trout
CÔTE DE PORC

My rules of thumb for aspiring chefs are: understand your ingredients, keep it simple, make it taste good. This dish is a relatively easy one to do, with not too many elements but lots of flavours which marry perfectly. For best results, brine your meats as it helps to tenderise and lock in flavour especially if you use herbs, spices and garlic. Brine this cut for 24 hours.

Preparation time: 30 minutes, plus 24 hours brining (optional) | Cooking time: 10 minutes | Serves: 2

Ingredients

For the remoulade:

½ small celeriac

45g mayonnaise

1 tsp wholegrain mustard

For the rösti:

1 large Marfona or Maris Piper potato (approx. 200g)

Few sprigs of thyme, leaves picked

Salt and pepper

1 tbsp each of duck fat and rapeseed oil

For the diced apple:

1 Granny Smith apple

Apple juice

For the wild garlic pesto:

15g each of fresh basil and wild garlic, roughly chopped

50g pine nuts

½ lemon, zested and juiced

3 tbsp olive oil

15g Parmesan, finely grated

Salt and freshly ground black pepper

For the cider gravy:

100ml each of Aspall's Cyder and cider vinegar

50g Demerara sugar

200ml good quality liquid chicken stock

For the côte de porc:

Knob of butter

Marmite (optional)

2 pork ribeye steaks on the bone, from your local butcher

Method

For the remoulade

To prepare the celeriac, peel and julienne or use a mandoline to chop into fine matchsticks. Cover the celeriac with salt and leave for 30 minutes. Squeeze out excess water using a clean tea towel. Combine the celeriac with the mayonnaise and mustard then season to taste. Keep at room temperature until serving.

For the rösti

Grate the potato and squeeze out any excess water, then mix with the thyme leaves, salt and pepper. Using 100mm shallow metal rings in a heavy frying pan, add the duck fat and oil and then put in a couple of heaped spoonfuls of grated potato. Gently press down to spread it out. Cook on a medium heat until one side turns golden, then remove the ring, flip and repeat on the other side. If you don't have a ring, just make a ball then flatten it like a patty before putting it in the pan.

For the diced apple

Peel and dice the apple into 10mm cubes and then place into apple juice to prevent the apple discolouring until needed.

For the wild garlic pesto

Grind the basil and wild garlic in a mortar with a pestle or blitz in a food processor to release the natural oils. Then add the pine nuts and lemon zest. Once combined, add the olive oil to make a paste and grind in the Parmesan. Add lemon juice and season to taste.

For the cider gravy

Place the cider, cider vinegar, and sugar in a pan and reduce by two thirds. Add the chicken stock, reduce by half again and your gravy is ready.

For the côte de porc

We use Marmite butter to baste the pork which is stunning. Just add Marmite to the butter according to your preference and brush the pork with it before and during cooking.

Put the pork onto a preheated griddle pan, occasionally turning it 45 degrees to create crossed lines throughout the cooking. Turn over after 3 minutes. Don't forget to brush the pork with the Marmite butter if using during cooking. Cook for approximately 6 minutes in total. Allow to rest for 4 minutes before serving.

To serve

Plate the rested pork, remoulade, rösti, diced apple, pesto and finish with the gravy. Add a couple of spears of asparagus or tenderstem broccoli depending on the season.

A roaring
SUCCESS

Friendly, family-oriented and full of great food; what's not to love about Great Longstone's independently run pub with bar and restaurant?

Greg and Libby Robinson own the White Lion, a stylish bar and restaurant in the friendly village of Great Longstone. Having come from a background in the hospitality industry, the husband and wife team took on the pub in 2009 and lovingly restored the interiors to create welcoming and cosy places to sit and enjoy a drink or a good meal.

The menus at the White Lion are full of traditional English favourites, with one or two surprises. Flatbread pizzas, burgers, pub classics and pasta dishes are all made in-house and some dishes have even been adapted so they can be enjoyed as a takeaway. There's also a Sunday lunch and three course evening menus, so whatever the occasion there's a great meal waiting. Greg is head chef and loves to use local food as well as employing local staff to work in the kitchen or front of house, which is managed by Libby.

The menus change every couple of months, and there's also a great selection of wines, beers and spirits at the bar. "People just want good food at a good price," says Greg, "and that's always what we aim for here." The kitchen team are keen to be very accommodating of dietary requirements, and go the extra mile to welcome families and even four-legged friends so everyone can visit. The White Lion can boast beautiful surroundings; being near to both Chatsworth and Bakewell means there are great walks to and from the pub to set you up for a hearty lunch or dinner.

Greg and Libby also own Harrow Cottage so visitors can stay and enjoy the beautiful area for longer. The luxury four star accommodation is also in the village of Great Longstone, not far from the White Lion, and has been restored – much like the pub – with love into a modern barn conversion with lots of character like its neighbour.

Events such as live jazz nights are occasionally held at the White Lion, and the rooms are perfect for hiring out if you're celebrating. Greg and Libby offer flexible options for people to party and enjoy bespoke sit-down meals. As the winner of Derbyshire Life's Best Dining Pub of the Year award, the White Lion has a warm welcome for everyone, whether you're popping in for a pint or indulging in a delicious freshly prepared meal.

White Lion
Great Longstone
TRIO OF FISH

This dish came about because two chefs could not agree on the fish choice for the new menu, so a little from both the ideas was used.

Preparation time: 1 hour | Cooking time: 15 minutes | Serves: 4

Ingredients

Salt and pepper

Bunch of fresh dill, finely chopped

For the crab cakes:

250g potatoes, peeled and diced

150g pasteurised crab meat

Plain flour

1 egg, beaten

50g breadcrumbs

For the aioli:

1 bulb of garlic

Pinch of saffron

3-4 tbsp mayonnaise

For the new potatoes:

1kg new potatoes

For the squid rings:

4 squid tubes

100g sweet chilli sauce

For the red mullet:

4 150g red mullet fillets (skin on)

To serve:

Vegetable oil

4 small side salads

1 lemon, sliced into wedges

Method

For the crab cakes

Boil the diced potatoes for about 15 minutes, drain and leave to steam dry for 5 minutes, and then mash. While the mash is still warm (not hot) add the crab meat, a pinch of salt and some of the fresh dill. Mix well, and make four croquette shapes. Place in the fridge. When firm, dust in flour, dip in beaten egg, let the excess drip off and then evenly coat in breadcrumbs before returning to the fridge.

For the aioli

Peel the garlic and place in a small saucepan with the saffron and 200ml of water. Simmer for 15 minutes or until the garlic is very soft and there's 50ml of water left. Place the garlic and water into a food processor with three tablespoons of mayonnaise, blend, and add a little more mayonnaise if the mixture is still runny. The aioli should be soft but spoonable. When the consistency is right, place into the fridge.

For the new potatoes

Boil the new potatoes for around 15 minutes until tender. Drain and leave for about 10 minutes so they are warm, not hot. Crush with the back of a spoon, add some chopped dill, a pinch of salt, and a twist of black pepper, then mix well. Lay out a large square of cling film and place the potato mix in a line in the centre. Roll up to form a thick sausage and place in the fridge. When chilled, slice into four thick rings, remove the cling film, and place the rounds on a lined baking tray.

For the squid rings

Slice the squid tubes into 1cm rings. Place in a pan of cold water, bring to the boil and then turn down the heat to cook gently. When the squid is easy to bite, transfer into cold water, and then drain when cold. Mix the squid rings with the sweet chilli sauce, place in a microwaveable tub and then leave in the fridge.

For the red mullet

Score the skin of the red mullet with a sharp knife to prevent it curling when cooking.

To serve

Place the new potato rings in a preheated oven at 180°c for 15 minutes. Add some vegetable oil to a cold non-stick pan and place the fillets of mullet skin side down into it. Cook on a low heat until the top of mullet turns white; about 15 minutes. Place the crab cakes into a small deep fat fryer until golden brown. Microwave the squid rings gently until warm. Serve on four large plates with the salad and lemon wedges.

The DIRECTORY

These great businesses have supported the making of this book; please support and enjoy them.

The Alphabet Gift Shop Burton

9-10 Union Street
Burton-on-Trent
Staffordshire
DE14 1AA
Telephone: 01283 749933

The Alphabet Gift Shop Mickleover

44 Station Road
Mickleover
Derby
DE3 9GH
Telephone: 01332 513033
Website:
www.thealphabetgiftshop.co.uk
Two gift shops with a wide selection of beautifully made, carefully chosen, design-led products which can be personalised at the Burton studio. Each location has a coffee shop serving freshly made food, drinks and irresistible cakes throughout the day.

The Bottle Kiln

High Lane West
West Hallam
Derbyshire
DE7 6HP
Telephone: 01159 329442
Website: www.bottlekiln.co.uk
Lifestyle shop with café and garden in a converted pottery; a tranquil retreat to indulge in and enjoy a unique contemporary space, good food and beautiful things.

The Bridge Bakehouse

42A Market Street
Whaley Bridge
High Peak
Derbyshire
SK23 7LP
Telephone: 01663 734113
Website:
www.thebridgebakehouse.co.uk
The Bridge Bakehouse is a beautiful family-run artisan patisserie and is the pride and joy of Whaley Bridge, Derbyshire.

Chatsworth Estate Farm Shop

Pilsley
Bakewell
Derbyshire
DE45 1UF
Telephone: 01246 565411
Website: www.chatsworth.org
The Chatsworth Estate Farm Shop showcases the very best in fresh meats, game, poultry and fish. It produces cooked meats, pies, breads and cakes in-house and champions the highest quality, mostly local, artisan products.

Chesterfield Markets

Markets Office
Market Hall
Chesterfield
S40 1AR
Telephone: 01246 345777
Website:
www.visitchesterfield.info/markets
There's plenty of produce, great bargains and memorable experiences all year round in Chesterfield at the open air market, flea market, farmers' market and Artisan Market that trade in the town centre.

Cow Close Farm

Birley Lane
Hathersage
Hope Valley
Derbyshire
S32 1DY
Telephone: 01433 659356
Website: www.cowclose.farm

Artisan cheesemakers by husband and wife team James and Sophie Summerlin, producing handmade cheese on their own farm beneath Stanage Edge in the Peak District.

The Elm Tree

Elmton
Worksop
Derbyshire
S80 4LS
Telephone: 01909 721261
Website: www.elmtreeelmton.co.uk

Picturesque and unpretentious country pub for eating out with friends, family and food lovers in the Derbyshire countryside.

EnergyBallRecipes.com

Telephone: 07966 279061
Website:
www.energyballrecipes.com

Energy Ball Recipe Kits have all the ingredients to make 30 healthy energy balls. Once made, they stay fresh in the fridge for seven days. Suitable for vegetarians and vegans. All packaging is eco-friendly.

Ferndale Garden and Home

Dyche Lane
Coal Aston
Dronfield
Derbyshire
S18 3BJ
Telephone: 01246 412763
Website:
www.ferndalegardencentre.co.uk

Ferndale Garden Centre's aim is 'to make your world more beautiful' and this frames everything when choosing plants, products and of course food for you to enjoy from the coffee shop.

Fintons Café & Bakehouse

29c Draycott Road
Breaston
DE72 3DA
Telephone: 01332 986556
Find us on Facebook @
FintonsBakehouse

Serving great coffee, lovely breakfasts, delicious lunches and tempting cakes made in-house with a large gluten- and dairy-free selection.

Fischer's Baslow Hall Limited

Calver Road
Baslow
Derbyshire
DE45 1RR
Telephone: 01246 583259
Website:
www.fischers-baslowhall.co.uk

Award-winning, individual, stylish, boutique country house hotel and restaurant on the edge of Baslow, with the glorious countryside of the Peak District on the doorstep.

Fredericks of Chesterfield Factory

76-88 Old Hall Road
Chesterfield
S401HF
Telephone: 01246 275293

Call for private bookings, parties, deliveries etc.

Queens Park Café & Gelateria

North Lodge
Queens Park
Chesterfield
S402LD
Telephone: 01246 563952

Bakewell Café & Gelateria

1 Bridge Street
Bakewell
DE452DS
Telephone: 01629 812849
Website:
www.fredericksicecreams.co.uk

Family ice cream makers with over 100 years of history, bringing award-winning ice cream made to the original 1898 recipe to Derbyshire through online delivery, a fleet of vans, and a café and gelateria in Bakewell and Queens Park, Chesterfield.

Fresh Basil

Strutt Street
Belper
Derbyshire
DE56 1UN
Telephone: 01773 828882
Website: www.freshbasil.co.uk

Award-winning deli and eatery celebrating Derbyshire produce, which you can take home or enjoy as a freshly prepared meal in rustic surroundings.

The George at Alstonefield

Alstonefield
Ashbourne
DE6 2FX
Telephone: 01335 310205
Website:
www.thegeorgeatalstonefield.com
Beautiful village pub with bar and restaurant; passionate about local produce, great food and drink, and a friendly welcome.

Ginger Butchers

Unit 2 Granby Road
Bakewell
DE45 1ES
Telephone: 01629 814280
Website:
www.gingerbutchers.co.uk
Family butchers and farmers.

Hassop Station Café

Hassop Road
Bakewell
DE45 1NW
Telephone: 01629 815668
Website: www.hassopstation.co.uk
Award-winning café on the stunning Monsal Trail in the heart of the Peak District. Food, family and fresh air!

Junction Bar

3 Chatsworth Road
Chesterfield
S40 2AH
Telephone: 01246 277911
Website: www.junctionbar.co.uk
Fun and friendly bar on Chesterfield's Brampton Mile serving cocktails, real ales, coffee and cake with regular live music and a warm welcome.

The Market Pub

95 New Square
Chesterfield
Derbyshire
S40 1AH
Telephone: 01246 273641
Website: www.themarketpub.co.uk
Traditional pub serving a wide selection of ale, whiskey, and wine alongside homemade food which includes lots of vegetarian and vegan options.

The Old Hall Inn & Paper Mill Inn

Whitehough
Chinley
SK23 6EJ
Telephone: 01663 750529
Website: www.old-hall-inn.co.uk
Traditional country inn hospitality, tastefully brought into the 21st century with a talented team of chefs, a great network of the best local suppliers and an impeccable drinks offer.

Original Recipes Ltd.

Unit 89 Circular Road
Storforth lane Trading Estate
Chesterfield
S41 0SN
Telephone: 01246 555497
Website: www.originalrecipes.co.uk
Original Recipes is a producer of the finest quality pâtés and terrines for the retail and catering market.

The Packhorse Inn

Main Street
Little Longstone
Bakewell
Derbyshire DE45 1NN
Telephone: 01629 640471
Website:
www.packhorselongstone.co.uk
Historic pub surrounded by some of the most striking scenery the Peak District has to offer; the perfect setting to enjoy real ales and locally sourced food.

The Peacock at Rowsley

Bakewell Road
Rowsley
DE4 2EB
Telephone: 01629 733518
Website:
www.thepeacockatrowsley.com
Boutique Peak District hotel with restaurant, located in the heart of Derbyshire on the Haddon Estate, close to both Bakewell and Chatsworth House.

Peak District Deli

Email: hello@peakdistrictdeli.com
Website: www.peakdistrictdeli.com
Telephone: Ralph 07778 702096
Lauren 07935 070147
Providing the best produce the Peak District has to offer through our online deli and in the menus we create for events, private dining and pop up supper clubs.

Rowley's Village Pub

Church Street
Baslow
DE45 1RY
Telephone: 01246 583880
Website:
www.rowleysvillagepub.co.uk
Rowley's sits on the edge of the beautiful Chatsworth Estate in the pretty village of Baslow. Our passion is fresh, seasonal food using local ingredients in an informal and relaxed atmosphere.

Teresa Lambarelli's Italian Caffe and Pasta Bar

7 Chatsworth Road
Chesterfield
Derbyshire
S40 2AH
Telephone: 01246 555516 /
07727 618741
Website:
www.teresalambarelli.co.uk
The home of award-winning pasta sauces and authentic Italian dining in the heart of Chesterfield.

The Tickled Trout

33 Valley Road,
Barlow,
Derbyshire
S18 7SL
Telephone: 01142 891111
Website:
www.tickledtroutbarlow.com
Deliciously Derbyshire sums up the pub restaurant, which sources and champions the best local and artisan produce and creates a relaxed dining environment with brilliantly executed food by a top team.

H&F Vintage Tearooms

4a New Beetwell Street
Chesterfield
S40 1QR
Telephone: 01246 556079
Website:
www.vintage-tearooms.co.uk
At Vintage Tearooms we offer an old fashioned setting and traditional treats so you can escape from the hustle and bustle of modern life.

The White Horse at Woolley Moor

Badger Lane
Woolley Moor
Derbyshire
DE55 6FG
Telephone: 01246 590319
Website: www.
thewhitehorsewoolleymoor.co.uk
Fresh food made with local produce, accommodation in the beautiful Derbyshire countryside and contemporary luxury at a welcoming country inn.

White Lion at Great Longstone

Main Street
Great Longstone
Bakewell
Derbyshire
DE45 1TA
Telephone: 01629 640252
Website: www.
whiteliongreatlongstone.co.uk
Stylish bar and restaurant in a friendly village with beautiful surroundings, serving a freshly prepared menu of favourites old and new.

Other titles in the 'Get Stuck In' series

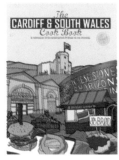

The Cardiff & South Wales Cook Book
features James Sommerin of Restaurant James Sommerin, Cocorico Patisserie, Sosban and lots more.
978-1-910863-31-2

The Cambridgeshire Cook Book: Second Helpings
features Mark Abbott of Midsummer House, The Olive Grove, Elder Street Café and lots more.
978-1-910863-33-6

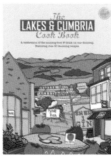

The Lakes & Cumbria Cook Book
features Simon Rogan's L'Enclume, Forest Side, Hawkshead Relish, L'al Churrasco and lots more.
978-1-910863-30-5

The Nottingham Cook Book: Second Helpings
features Welbeck Estate, Memsaab, Sauce Shop, 200 Degrees Coffee, Homeboys, Rustic Crust and lots more.
978-1-910863-27-5

The Devon Cook Book
sponsored by Food Drink Devon features Simon Hulstone of The Elephant, Noel Corston, Riverford Field Kitchen and much more.
978-1-910863-24-4

The South London Cook Book
features Jose Pizarro, Adam Byatt, The Alma, Piccalilli Caff, Canopy Beer, Inkspot Brewery and lots more.
978-1-910863-27-5

The Brighton & Sussex Cook Book features Steven Edwards, The Bluebird Tea Co, Isaac At, Real Patisserie, Sussex Produce Co, and lots more.
978-1-910863-22-0

The Liverpool Cook Book
features Burnt Truffle, The Art School, Fraîche, Villaggio Cucina and many more.
978-1-910863-15-2

The Bristol Cook Book
features Dean Edwards, Lido, Clifton Sausage, The Ox, and wines from Corks of Cotham plus lots more.
978-1-910863-14-5

The Leeds Cook Book
features The Boxtree, Crafthouse, Stockdales of Yorkshire and lots more.
978-1-910863-18-3

The Cotswolds Cook Book
features David Everitt-Matthias of Champignon Sauvage, Prithvi, Chef's Dozen and lots more.
978-0-9928981-9-9

The Shropshire Cook Book
features Chris Burt of The Peach Tree, Old Downton Lodge, Shrewsbury Market, CSons and lots more.
978-1-910863-32-9

The Norfolk Cook Book
features Richard Bainbridge, Morston Hall, The Duck Inn and lots more.
978-1-910863-01-5

The Essex Cook Book features Thomas Leatherbarrow, The Anchor Riverside, Great Garnetts, Deersbrook Farm, Mayfield Bakery and lots more.
978-1-910863-25-1

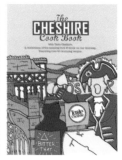

The Cheshire Cook Book
features Simon Radley of The Chester Grosvenor, The Chef's Table, Great North Pie Co., Harthill Cookery School and lots more.
978-1-910863-07-7

All books in this series are available from Waterstones, Amazon and independent bookshops.

FIND OUT MORE ABOUT US AT WWW.MEZEPUBLISHING.CO.UK